Contents

Mackenzie Crook

Foreword

ORDNANCE SURVEY
Scale 1:25,000 or about 2½ Inches to 1 Mile
Provisional Edition

"Danebury TL91"

In publicity interviews for the first series of *Detectorists*, I remember claiming that the whole process—from the initial idea, to getting it commissioned, shot, and onto the screen—had been refreshingly swift, at just over eighteen months. It was only when I started writing the second series, and looking back through old notebooks for discarded ideas, that I found the concept sketched out over three pages in an entry from 1999. I was stunned to realise I had the idea nearly fifteen years previously and had left it to percolate until the time was right.

On the first of those pages I had written the title, *The Metal Detectors* (rooky mistake, embarrassing…), followed by vague notions of two men talking rubbish in a field, and a "Treasurecam" that allowed viewers to see what the characters couldn't.

Back then I hadn't yet realised it was a comedy, and the two central characters were far more mercenary and were in the hobby to get rich. (A brief remnant of that remains in the very first episode, when Lance chides Andy for not selling his finds on eBay. That line jars with me now as we know Lance better and know that's not his style.)

The programme was initially a lot bleaker too. The best metal detecting is to be had on arable land, tilled for centuries, trodden by generations, that, with every ploughing, brings more relics to the surface. As such, most real-life detecting happens in the autumn and winter months when fields are fallow. It's a much colder, wetter, and far more gruelling hobby than we portray in the programme. The ideal ground conditions are hardly ever encountered, being either too hard to dig (I once soaked a football-sized hunk of earth in water for an hour to get at a shotgun cap) or so wet that your boots collect several pounds of mud every few yards. In that decade-and-a-half of subliminal pondering, the programme turned into a comedy; the sun came out and Lance and Andy became far more pleasant and likeable.

A significant event that occurred during that long incubation period was a glorious new play in which I was cast and performed over four hundred times in the West End and on Broadway. *Jerusalem*, by Jez Butterworth, was a modern play set in rural Wiltshire that spoke about giants and ghosts and ancient, pagan gods. Although so much has been written since about *Jerusalem*, I still struggle to explain, to those who didn't see it, exactly what it's about. But during rehearsals we steeped ourselves in the myth and lore of the English landscape and I know that, during that time, many seeds were planted that eventually grew into the ideas discussed in these pages.

As is mentioned in this book, soon after *Detectorists* was commissioned I got a job in Canada and most of the writing was done in a glass high-rise in downtown Vancouver. I didn't enjoy that job and longed to get back home. I remember one time a small bird flew past my tenth-storey window and I leapt up to see it, so starved was I of any element of the natural world. I watched as the little finch zipped away, high above the traffic and flew smack into the mirrored glass of the building opposite, from where it plummeted to the pavement. It was about the saddest thing I've ever seen.

But perhaps that longing for home informed some of the romantic ideas of landscape and what it means to each of us, and maybe *Detectorists* wouldn't have turned out the same if I'd written it anywhere else.

The idea for *Detectorists* changed and evolved over time, to a large extent subconsciously, and many of the themes mentioned in this book also seeped in there largely without my realising. To have them explored in these wonderful essays was quite a revelation, I found myself reading things that I *kind* of knew, but didn't *realise* I knew until they were pointed out, which made me feel very clever and pretty stupid at the same time. As far as I'm concerned, the writers have understood *Detectorists* more fully than I ever have, and that's fine.

I'd never tried metal detecting before I wrote *Detectorists*, although the idea had always fascinated me. Once I purchased my first detector, it wasn't long before I was hooked, even if all I was finding were buttons and "can-slaw". I secured permission to detect on a farm in Suffolk and slowly I got better and my finds more interesting. One discovery made it into the first episode of the third series. I was detecting on my own (a bit like the Lone Ranger, Hugh, yeah), and dug down four inches to find an exquisite bronze hawking whistle. I took a few minutes to unclog the mud with a piece of straw, then held it to my lips and

"The note that issued from the whistle was a ghost, a sound unheard for centuries"

blew. The note that issued from the whistle was a ghost, a sound unheard for centuries, and the last person to hear that sound, that *exact* sound, was the person who dropped it just yards from where I was standing. And it wasn't a faint, feeble ghost either: it was an urgent, piercing shrill that echoed across the field and back through time.

A year later, very close to that spot, I found my gold: a piece of Roman jewellery, an earring or pendant embossed with a long-necked bird design. Some time later, it was officially declared treasure by the British Museum and, with that, I felt like my metal detecting was over; I'm glad I don't *have* to do it like Andy and Lance. But my fascination with the English landscape is enduring, and I feel my business there is not yet done. My next project is also set in the countryside amongst nature, myth, and legend. I only hope the authors of this book will be on hand afterwards to analyse it and tell me exactly what it is I've done.

Thank you to Adam Tandy who helped collate my scattered thoughts and create the world of Danebury and to Gill Isles who took the producing reins and steered us through the third series. And thank you to Innes, Isla, Andrew, and Joanne for writing this book. That you've taken time to study and analyse *Detectorists* so thoroughly and with such good humour is a huge compliment.

"Detectorists *enfolds a non-human supporting cast of insects, birds, plants, and trees*"

Innes M. Keighren & Joanne Norcup

Introduction

1. Robert Lloyd, 'British *Detectorists* on Acorn TV uncovers a comedy treasure', *Los Angeles Times*, 25 August 2015: latimes.com/entertainment/tv/la-et-st-detectorists-interview-20150824-column.html; Jamie Fewery, '*Detectorists* teaches us everything we need to know about male friendship', *The Daily Telegraph*, 29 October 2015: telegraph.co.uk/men/thinking-man/11961154/*Detectorists*-teaches-us-everything-we-need-to-know-about-male-friendship.html

2. SumsionMichael, 5 October 2014: twitter.com/SumsionMichael/status/518852506194305025

3. Rachel Meaden, 'The quiet brilliance of Mackenzie Crook's *Detectorists*', *Den of Geek*, 23 December 2015: denofgeek.com/tv/detectorists/38300/the-quiet-brilliance-of-mackenzie-crooks-detectorists

4. Chas 'n' Dave, *Harry Was A Champion*, 1984.

5. Andy Medhurst, *A National Joke: Popular Comedy and English Cultural Identities* (London: Routledge, 2007).

6. Phil Emmerson, 'From Coping to Carrying On: A Pragmatic Laughter Between Life and Death', *Transactions of the Institute of British Geographers* 44, no.1 (2019); Patricia Noxolo, *Fleshy Textuality: Caribbean Laughter, Bodies and Texts* (Liverpool: Liverpool University Press, forthcoming).

7. David Matless, *Landscape and Englishness* (London: Reaktion, 1998 and 2016). See, also, Sean J. Nixon, 'Vanishing Peregrines: J. A. Baker, Environmental Crisis and Bird-Centred Cultures of Nature, 1954–73', *Rural History* 28, no.2 (2017).

8. On geographical engagements with amateur enthusiasm and citizen science, respectively, see Ruth Craggs, Hilary Geoghegan, and Hannah Neate, 'Architectural Enthusiasm: Visiting Buildings with The Twentieth Century Society', *Environment and Planning D: Society and Space* 31, no.5 (2013); and Hilary Geoghegan, Alison Dkye, Rachel Pateman, Sara West, and Glyn Everett, *Understanding Motivations for Citizen Science* (Swindon: UK Environmental Observation Framework, 2016).

9. We would like to thank the Historical Geography Research Group and the Social and Cultural Geography Research Group for jointly sponsoring the session.

Across three series and a Christmas special (2014–17), the BAFTA-award-winning situation comedy-drama *Detectorists* has garnered critical praise for its portrayal of metal detecting and amateur archaeology in rural England. In its attention to the embodied practice of detecting, and to the social worlds of detectorists, the programme has been described by critics variously as "about hardly anything and almost everything" and "the most accurate portrait of men being men that you'll find in current popular culture".[1] For one Twitter user, the show is simply "a warm, beguiling, slow-burn meditation on male friendship and prosaic details of Englishness, plus some metal".[2] Nuanced characterisation and relatable situations have endeared *Detectorists* to viewers in the United Kingdom and beyond who have praised the programme's "humanity and the honest observations of the real world".[3]

This book came into being in a slow, organic fashion. Two friends who share a professional interest in historical geography and a personal passion for the history of comedy found themselves discussing *Detectorists* increasingly frequently after the first episode was broadcast in October 2014. By the time the second series had completed its first run in 2015, we were both assured that there was something that we—as 'Geography Degrees'—wanted to say about *Detectorists*. The programme struck a chord with us for several reasons: it spoke to the significance of the rural environment at a time of ecological crisis; it highlighted a popular desire for stillness and gentleness in an era of acceleration and anxiety; and it told us something about contested notions of Englishness during a period of increasing political polarisation. In resonating with the present, *Detectorists* seems also to speak to the future: it is a gift by which those who are yet to come will understand something of the cultures of Englishness in the early twenty-first century.

The book offers four distinct geographical readings of *Detectorists*: Innes M. Keighren attends to the sensory, technological, and emotional interpretation of landscape; Isla Forsyth examines the relationship between objects, memory, and place; the significance of verticality, the aerial, and groundedness is discussed by Andrew Harris; and Joanne Norcup considers the contested interconnections of gender, expertise, and knowledge making. The collection is bookended by reflections on the creative processes and decisions that supported the journey of *Detectorists* from script to screen: in the foreword written by its writer-director, Mackenzie Crook, and in the afterword written by its originating producer, Adam Tandy. In what follows, we introduce three themes that cut across the book's analytical chapters: comedy as a cultural medium that can permit different forms of geographical analysis; the relationship between landscape and forms of identity and belonging; and the role of hobbies in defining senses of identity, community, and purpose.

Comedy geographies and the geographies of popular comedy

Popular comedy too often gets overlooked by academic researchers working outside film and television studies: an omission predicated either on the assumption that popular comedy as a medium equates simply to humour—and a lack of seriousness of purpose—or, to quote Cockney folk duo Chas 'n' Dave, that it is seen by "academicals" as "[not] quite the proper thing".[4] Comedy as a cultural art form has the power, however, to transform our inner worlds and outer perspectives, both emotionally and cognitively: to hold a mirror up to contemporary issues and to subvert, satirise, and challenge dominant narratives and moralities.[5]

While geographers have attended in recent years to the emotional importance of laughter and humour, and comedy as a medium for postcolonial discussions of identity, popular television situation comedies have rarely featured as a focus for explicit geographical analysis.[6] This book aims to correct that oversight, not by imposing academic ideas onto comedy, but rather by drawing out the geographical resonances from one production—*Detectorists*, in this case—in order to show how geographical ideas and themes such as landscape, memory, gender, and identity are articulated variously through script and dialogue, costume and performance, set and location, and cinematography and sound. What we hope this book will do is give geographers the permission to take comedy seriously and, in doing so, to illustrate how geographical forms of investigation and analysis can help us understand the cultural value of comedy in all its rich complexity.

Landscapes and the geographical imagination

Detectorists is distinct from most situation comedies in that much of the action takes place outdoors: in the fields and meadows where the programme's protagonists pursue their hobby. While some spaces are more traditionally 'sitcom'— the inside of Lance's flat or Andy's home, for example—other locations serve to showcase the wider community: the Scout hut that hosts the Tuesday-evening meetings of the Danebury Metal Detecting Club (DMDC) and the Two Brewers pub where post-meeting analysis takes place. For the most part, however, *Detectorists* is situated out there: in fields of low crop stubble where the bleep and chatter of detectors echoes the background call of birds, or under the shelter of an ancient oak tree, where sandwiches are unwrapped and Thermos flasks of coffee decanted.

Landscape is, however, more than simply a setting: it is the focus of the protagonists' preoccupations. In *Detectorists*, the landscape is variously walked, surveyed, sensed, gazed upon, read, and dug. Landscape is where the programme's characters seek solitude, find companionship, and navigate the sometimes-dramatic intrusions from 'the rude world'. Landscape reveals the past while concealing the prospect of future discovery. Landscape in *Detectorists* also shifts in its historical focus and geographical scale in response to the programme's dramatic tensions and trajectories: the first series recalls the landscapes of Saxon England as Lance and Andy seek out the burial place of Sexred, king of the East Saxons; the second series makes international connections as Andy considers the prospect of archaeological work in Botswana and the DMDC comes to the assistance of a German detectorist, Peter, who is searching for the remains of his grandfather's aeroplane, shot down over Danebury during the Second World War; and the third series considers landscapes of rural modernity as the DMDC races to find gold before its detecting site is lost to a new solar farm. Landscape in *Detectorists* is simultaneously local and global, of now and of the past and the future.

Aesthetically and thematically, landscape dominates *Detectorists*. Filmed in and around Framlingham, Suffolk—standing in for Essex, and the fictional town of Danebury—the visual palette of the programme echoes the landscape paintings of Thomas Gainsborough and Peter Hall's 1974 cinematic rendering of Ronald Blythe's book *Akenfield* (1969) while, at the same time, enfolding a non-human supporting cast of insects, birds, plants, and trees. While unmistakably a rural landscape, Danebury and its surroundings are not falsely bucolic, but are rendered as recognisably twenty-first century. The camera lingers at one point on an empty sauce pot as it eddies with the breeze on the surface of a murky roadside puddle—a reminder that not all is pure and natural in the countryside. The efforts on the part of Hugh and Russell to recover the mayor's chain of office, lost in a renowned dogging area, likewise echo the work of artist George Shaw, particularly his *My Back to Nature* series of paintings (2017) that document the material and moral detritus of human presence in woodlands and undergrowth: discarded bras and bottles, wooden pallets and dustbin bags, mouldering pornographic magazines and trees disfigured with graffiti phalluses. Such juxtapositions remind us that the rural is still, messily, an inhabited landscape.

In *Detectorists*, we also see a landscape that is populated —and made sense of—by bodies in pursuit of leisure and connection with nature: not just the titular detectorists, but also ramblers, bird watchers, and conservationists. Reflecting a longer tradition of amateur naturalism and rural leisure, these activities, often undertaken as part of a club or society, are predicated upon curiosity and discovery—they create the opportunity for new ways of seeing and knowing the world and serve to build communities in and through place.[7] These amateur and leisure-based ways of being in, valuing, and making knowledge about place and location have contemporary parallels in efforts to engage the public as citizen scientists.[8]

"Not all is pure and natural in the countryside"

Hobby geographies

Significant to the success of *Detectorists* is the attention that is devoted to its protagonists' pursuit of their hobby. As contemporary landscapes of employment become ever more challenging, with increasing job precarity and the rise of the so-called gig economy, hobbies and pastimes arguably assume a greater significance in the construction of individuals' senses of identity and purpose; people's passions and dedications come to define who they are more than do their careers or working lives. In *Detectorists*, metal detecting is not mined for cheap laughs, rather it is presented as the social mechanism that connects individuals with those who share their passions and interests and who see value in a set of skills and abilities cultivated and deployed outside the context of work. Here, we see that hobbies gift people their humanity and speak in important ways to their fundamental desires and aspirations.

The idea of the book

This book began with our appreciation of *Detectorists* and evolved to become our hobby: a passion project from which we drew both value and pleasure. It was a hobby that also connected us with others who shared our enthusiasm for the programme: its engagement with landscape, its ecological resonances, its attention to place and identity. Unexpectedly, we found a community of academics brought together by a sitcom. In lieu of a Scout hut in which to hold a meeting of our nascent club, we instead organised a paper session at the Annual International Conference of the Royal Geographical Society (with the Institute of British Geographers) in Cardiff in 2018 and circulated a call for papers.[9] We knew from comments made by other academics that our session was seen as somewhat 'experimental' and a little risky. It smacked of fandom; our passions perhaps too exposed. Happily, however, papers came in from a number of academics—including Isla Forsyth and Andrew Harris—who saw in *Detectorists* a rich resource for geographical analysis and commentary. Buoyed by this response, we invited

Adam Tandy, producer of the first two series of *Detectorists*, to act as discussant for the session—an offer he kindly accepted. The stage was thus set for our first meeting. Andrew sourced and wore a camouflage shirt in keeping with the spirit of the programme. Joanne set up a mock 'finds table' with homemade pin badges bearing images of characters from *Detectorists* which audience members could buy (with all donations going to the Bat Conservation Trust). This was a DMDC rally cum academic conference session.

It was a risk. We risked failing, we risked looking foolish, we risked being seen as unscholarly. It was, however, an experiment that worked, in no small part due to the large and engaged audience who came ready to take comedy seriously. And when subsequently Colin Sackett, publisher of Uniformbooks, approached us to turn the session's papers into this book, we had to say yes. Later, when Mackenzie Crook agreed to write a foreword for the book, we knew that the project had been a risk worth taking. We felt as though we had struck gold.

Writing this book has become more than simply an exercise in dovetailing our geographical interests with our appreciation for *Detectorists*: it has provided, for all its contributors, an escape from the dominant modes of academic production that see value only in certain forms of knowledge making and only in certain types of writing. This book has allowed us to reconnect with slower, more collegial, and ultimately more joyful ways of academic working. We have been enriched by the book and it has enriched the work we do beyond it. We hope you enjoy reading it as much as we have enjoyed writing it.

"When I look at this landscape, I can read it"

Innes M. Keighren

"When I look at this landscape, I can read it"—practices of landscape interpretation in *Detectorists*

1. Alan R. H. Baker, *Geography and History: Bridging the Divide* (Cambridge: Cambridge University Press, 2003); Matthew Johnson, *Ideas of Landscape* (Oxford: Blackwell, 2007); David Matless, 'One Man's England: W. G. Hoskins and the English Culture of Landscape', *Rural History* 4, no.2 (1993).
2. Richard Muir, *Approaches to Landscape* (Basingstoke: Macmillan, 1999): p.27.
3. W. G. Hoskins, *The Making of the English Landscape* (London: Hodder and Stoughton, 1955): p.14.
4. Hoskins, *English Landscape*, p.232, p.235.
5. Trevor Rowley, *The English Landscape in the Twentieth Century* (London: Hambledon Continuum, 2006): p.xii.
6. David Matless, 'Doing the English Village, 1945–90: An Essay in Imaginative Geography', in *Writing the Rural: Five Cultural Geographies*, Paul Cloke, Marcus Doel, David Matless, Martin Phillips, and Nigel Thrift (London: Paul Chapman, 1994): p.28.
7. Keith D. Lilley and Gareth Dean, 'A Silent Witness? Medieval Urban Landscapes and Unfolding their Mapping Histories', *Journal of Medieval History* 41, no.3 (2015): p.274, p.284.
8. Jane Struthers, *Red Sky at Night: The Book of Lost Country Wisdom* (London: Ebury, 2009).
9. *Detectorists*, Series (S) 1, Episode (E) 1, 7:16. / 10. S1, E5, 12:17. / 11. S1, E2, 15:51. / 12. S3, E1, 4:06. / 13. S1, E5, 12:33; S1, E1, 7:15. / 14. S1, E1, 14:44. / 15. S1, E1, 14:55. / 16. S1, E1, 14:58. / 17. S1, E1, 15:38. / 18. S1, E1, 15:42. / 19. S1, E1, 15:43. / 20. S1, E1, 15:54. / 21. S1, E1, 15:55. / 22. S1, E1, 15:57. / 23. S1, E1, 16:07. / 24. S1, E1, 16:18.
25. Denis Cosgrove and William L. Fox, *Photography and Flight* (London: Reaktion Books, 2010): p.9.
26. S1, E2, 18:11. / 27. S1, E2, 18:25. / 28. S1, E2, 22:45. / 29. S1, E2, 22:58. / 30. S1, E2, 23:04. / 31. S1, E2, 23:07. / 32. S1, E2, 23:09. / 33. S1, E2, 23:14. / 34. S1, E2, 22:54, 23:17. / 35. S3, E6, 26:34.
36. *Detectorists* shooting script, S3, E6, 14 June 2017: p.36.
37. S1, E6, 16:41. / 38. S1, E6, 16:48. / 39. S1, E6, 17:03. / 40. S1, E6, 17:06. / 41. S1, E6, 17:07.
42. *Detectorists* shooting script, S1, E6, 22 May 2014: p.23.
43. S1, E6, 18:06. / 44. S1, E6, 26:25.
45. *Detectorists* shooting script, S1, E6, 22 May 2014: p.31.

Among the rich and diverse twentieth-century literature on the nascent discipline of landscape history, W. G. Hoskins's *The Making of the English Landscape* (1955) is often considered canonical.[1] In that text, Hoskins "captured and conveyed a sense of countrysides that were alive with messages that could be read by initiates into the craft of the landscape historian".[2] Indeed, as Hoskins sought to persuade his readers, "The English landscape itself, to those who know how to read it aright, is the richest historical record we possess. There are discoveries to be made in it for which no written documents exist, or have ever existed."[3] Hoskins's argument was one, in effect, for topographical exegesis—for the idea that what the landscape presented to the eye of the viewer was, in its arrangement, composition, and features, a text from which the human and environmental history of that place could be read. For Hoskins, the modern English landscape (where it had not been denuded by the actions of "the scientist, the military men, and the politicians", whom he considered vandals) was the legacy of an ancient and persistent accretional process—the laying down of the "cultural humus of sixty generation or more".[4] Hoskins's palimpsestic understanding of the landscape, one partly informed by the earlier work of Lewis Mumford, was to treat the earth's surface as a layered record of cultural activity "on to which each generation writes its own story while at the same time erasing parts of the remnants of earlier stories".[5] Landscape was, for Hoskins, the outcome of an ever-iterating sequence of material additions and eliminations.

Although aspects of Hoskins's book have been subject to criticism—partly because of his resolutely "anti-progressive and anti-modern outlook" and partly because of his lack of engagement with the complementary and contemporaneous work of geographers—the work's influence on the academic and amateur study of landscape has been significant.[6] Across various scholarly disciplines, it is now recognised that "landscapes are silent witnesses imprinted upon by past local events" and that through particular methods of interpretation and investigation, one can succeed in "reading a landscape's testimony".[7] Beyond the academy, a plethora of popular how-to guides now offer visitors to the British countryside with advice on how to decipher the historical clues written into its landscapes. Capitalising on the wider popularity of contemporary nature writing, books such as Tristan Gooley's *The Walker's Guide to Outdoor Clues and Signs* (2014) and Mary-Ann Ochota's *Hidden Histories: A Spotter's Guide to the British Landscape* (2018), encourage readers to cast a fresh eye on otherwise familiar environments and, in so doing, to become attuned to the stories they are capable of telling. Such guidebooks seek to satisfy a desire among readers for a connection with the natural environment and hold the promise of restoring a rural lore and wisdom often thought lost or diminished by contemporary urban life.[8]

The methodological legacy of Hoskins is writ large in *Detectorists*; at various points in the series we see the protagonists enacting (with more or less success) various means of landscape interpretation in their quest for productive search areas. The detectorists rely variously on sight and survey, on instinct and tacit knowledge, and on maps and printed texts to guide their reading of landscape. At the same time, the metal detector itself is shown to be an instrument by which the landscape's "silent witness" is made audible—variously as beeps, shrieks, grunts, and chirps—and by which the past is made to speak to the present. In *Detectorists*, landscape is both read and heard.

This chapter takes as its focus the practices of landscape reading employed by the programme's lead characters in their attempts, during the first series, to locate the burial place of Sexred, king of the East Saxons. These practices reveal a tension between a belief that reading landscape is a tacit skill based upon instinct and in-the-field experience, and the pragmatic realisation that it might usefully be supplemented by particular visual technologies, such as Google Earth and Ordnance Survey maps. Underpinning this tension is a particular epistemological question about whose knowledge is most valuable in locating the hoped-for burial site: the instinctive sense of Lance and Andy, the titular detectorists, or the academic-disciplinary perspectives of Andy's geography-graduate girlfriend, Becky, and of Sophie, a new recruit to the DMDC and a student of ancient history at the local university. Reading landscape is shown to be, at turns, a subjective undertaking (drawing on experience and emotion) and an objective enterprise (depending upon rationality, detachment,

"This is the land of the Saxons. I wanna discover where they buried their warriors and their kings"

"Course, it's ninety percent instinct"

and distance). As a process of knowledge making, landscape interpretation is shown to require the application either of wisdom or deductive reasoning.

Surveying the deep past

The narrative arc of the first series of *Detectorists* is provided by Lance and Andy's twin search for treasure and for certainty in their respective personal relationships. Both are convinced that a Saxon ship burial must exist in Essex and that it is theirs to discover if only they can find the right location and secure the necessary permissions. "This is the land of the Saxons", Andy tells Becky; "I wanna discover where they buried their warriors and their kings".[9] Lance and Andy are driven by a desire to *make* history with a big discovery—to find their very own Sutton Hoo—but also to connect with history, to the deep past of the English landscape. Metal detecting is, as it were, a pastime built upon the prospect of encounters with a past time. As Lance tells Sophie, what they are searching for is "something that's been held by a Saxon or a Roman, [or] one of the other ancient peoples that once roamed this land before us".[10] Their search is, then, as much about reaching out across time, of walking in the footsteps of those who have gone before them, as it is about the prospect of material discovery itself. But where to start looking?

"Course, it's ninety percent instinct", Lance says, somewhat boastfully, as he holds court at a meeting of the DMDC.[11] Despite "swinging" the club's highest-specification detector (the Minelab CTX 3030, funded by a lottery win), Lance places apparently greater faith in the tacit knowledge he has developed through years of in-the-field experience. Lance is confident in his ability to make sense of what he sees: "You know", he tells Andy in the first episode of the programme's third series, "when I look at this landscape, I can read it. That's the likely site of a settlement. That's where the workers gather for their lunch."[12] Part of the programme's comedy comes, of course, from the fact that its protagonists have so routinely been *unsuccessful* in their searching; despite having "pulled a couple of tons of metal out of this county", all Lance and Andy seem to find is "litter and ring pulls".[13] Increasingly convinced of the value of a more systematic approach to identifying the likely site of the Saxon ship burial, Lance and Andy turn to technology and to text in their efforts to read the landscape for clues as to what might lie beneath its surface.

In the programme's first episode, Lance is convinced that he's made an important discovery using the aerial perspective provided by Google Earth and is keen to share his findings with Andy. Having polished off a vegetable curry, the two gather round Lance's laptop somewhat conspiratorially as Lance points out what it is that has caught his eye: "You know those cabbage fields off the B1010?", Lance asks, "Well, look at this. Ring-shaped feature in the field".[14] Andy is intrigued. "Iron-Age roundhouse", Lance concludes.[15] "But wait. There's more. Move to the left and voila... another one. But move again to the left... and here's yet another, slightly larger, circular feature. But this is different. This one has a some sort of entrance leading to an enclosure, a gateway. All in a line. Iron-Age settlement."[16] While Lance sees evidence of ancient occupation in these faint markings on the land, Andy can see them for what they really are: "Do these 'features' seem to spell anything?", he asks.[17] "No", Lance responds dismissively.[18] "Wait. Uh... G-O-O. Oh, fuck it."[19] "Do they seem to spell 'Google'?", Andy asks, just managing to keep a straight face.[20] Lance is instantaneously deflated: "Fuck it!", he says again.[21] He can see it clearly now: "It's the Google Earth water mark", he concedes.[22] Andy, who admits to having made the same mistake himself, spares Lance's blushes by returning their focus to the screen: "No, look, tell you where we wanna be. I've been doing my own recon... Look. This farm here."[23] He points, finding his target. "Look, this is the original Roman road, running up the side. Where you've got Roman, who's to say you haven't got Saxon as well? We all know there's a Saxon ship burial somewhere in this part of the county. We just gotta find it first."[24]

Here, the cartographical view from above has allowed Lance and Andy to see the familiar—their part of the county—in a new way: to read the commonplace landscape with fresh eyes and to interpret its significance in ways that on-the-ground observation might not permit. As Lance's recent experience

"You know those cabbage fields off the B1010? Well, look at this. Ring-shaped feature in the field"

"I'm not convinced they were buried here. Bede says that Sexred and his brother went *to fight the West Saxons*"

with Google Earth makes clear, however, it is a perspective that can also be misleading; being able to see the landscape from above is no guarantee of being able to make sense of it. Whether tracing the route of a Roman road or the misleading outline of the Google Earth watermark, both Lance and Andy are interrogating a palimpsest: a landscape whose story has been written and rewritten, layer upon layer, in both material and virtual space. All these inscriptions matter to the story the landscape is capable of telling; not all of them, however, are equally significant in guiding the protagonists' search. The God's-Eye perspective of aerial photography—whilst notionally capturing a single moment in time; the instant of the camera's shutter opening—has the uncanny capacity, through revealing features in the landscape otherwise unintelligible from ground level, to bring "historically distant… events into present place and time with astonishing verisimilitude".[25] As the detectorists' experience makes clear, however, being able to see through time depends upon understanding the language in which the landscape's story is written.

Authority and expertise

The authority of one's own eyewitness is not, however, all that matters in knowing where to search. When Sophie asks Andy why he is so convinced that Sexred is buried in Essex, Andy replies "We *know* he's around here. Bede says so in *Historia Ecclesiastica*".[26] When Sophie responds with surprise that Andy has read the Venerable Bede—rather than, say, Wikipedia— he is mildly offended: "you can learn a lot from the amateurs. We're the most passionate, the plebs".[27] Andy's lay reading of Bede is, however, later challenged by Sophie, the student of ancient history, who offers an alternative interpretation: "I'm not convinced he's buried here", she tells Andy and Lance.[28] "Bede says that Sexred and his brothers *went* to fight the West Saxons. They were *slain* in Wessex".[29] "Yeah", Lance retorts, "then they brought the *body* back here".[30] For Sophie, the facts are clear: "The army was completely destroyed, there was nobody left".[31] "Well", Lance insists, "a couple of them carried the corpse *here*".[32] "I don't buy it", Sophie concludes.[33] It eventually becomes clear that Lance's certainty is based not on his own reading of Bede, whom he considers "overrated", but on viewing "a documentary on *Discovery* presented by... Charlie off of *Casualty*".[34] There is, of course, an obvious joke here about authority and credibility, about who is a reliable guide to the landscape (the actor Derek Thompson or the chronicler Bede) and about whose knowledge, academic or lay, is to be trusted. What this exchange really points to, however, is the faith placed by the detectorists in their instinctive sense of history and place—about the story they desperately *want* to believe is true.

It is on this particular history of place (that here lies Sexred, king of the East Saxons), that the detectorists' future fulfilment is seen to depend. Over time, Lance and Andy have repeatedly laid down their own narrative onto the landscape that surrounds them: another layer in the palimpsest of place that has written their part of the county into a larger national-historical story and that promises them an important personal achievement should they find their treasure. Attentiveness to the storying of place is, indeed, something that the detectorists see as setting them apart, as hobbyists, from the academic interpretative approach applied by archaeologists. Towards the end of the third series, Lance reflects on that difference in approach: for him, archaeologists "gather up the facts, piece the jigsaw together", whilst detectorists "unearth the scattered memories, mine the stories, fill in the personality".[35] The shooting script makes this commitment to narrative clearer still: "we are story tellers", Lance tells Andy.[36] It is the story—written and read—that matters.

By means both visual and textual, Lance and Andy identify the specific part of the landscape where they might fulfil their destiny, and succeed in securing permission to detect there from the somewhat mercurial and unhinged landowner, Larry Bishop. As the series follows their largely unsuccessful and increasingly frustrating investigation of Bishop's farm, already twice dug by professional archaeologists, there is a growing sense that they might not be looking in the right place after all—that they might have misread the clues in the landscape. When Becky questions the wisdom of searching a site "that's twice

"If you're talking about a high-status royal Saxon ship burial, it would have been on the highest point of the landscape"

"I see what you're saying… It's interesting, certainly"

been searched but yielded nothing", Andy throws the challenge back to her: "All right, geography degree, where should we be searching?"[37]

Becky, Andy, Lance, and Sophie are in the Two Brewers pub, gathered round a 1:25,000 scale Ordnance Survey map of Danebury and its surroundings (in cartographic reality, the town of Maldon in Essex). The stage is thus set for Becky to read the landscape as a geographer. "Well", she begins, "If you're talking about a high-status royal Saxon ship burial, it would have been on the highest point of the landscape with clear views of the sea, which is this point here", her finger touching the centre point of a whorl of contour lines.[38] "But you can't see the sea from Bishop's farm", Sophie interjects.[39] "You can't now", Becky explains with a school-teacher's patience.[40] "In Elizabethan times pine woodlands were planted which thrive in this naturally acidic soil but in the sixth and seventh centuries that same soil would have meant hardly any native trees at all, giving clear views all the way to Southey Creek in the east, and the River Crouch in the south. And look", she says, getting into her flow, "you can't see it now coz a lot of this land has been built up or forested but clear away all these features and look—look at the natural contours, there's a clear passage. They would have sailed the ship up the river to this point here, taken it out of the water, and brought it up the valley to this point... here."[41] Her finger taps a point—what the shooting script identifies as "High Field", but what is, in cartographic reality, Loddart's Hill.[42] Becky's audience responds initially with awed silence. Lance, clearly unwilling to admit that he has misread the testimony of the landscape's topography, vegetation, and soil, concedes only that Becky's reading is "interesting".[43] Nevertheless, the group scramble to their feet, leaving their pints unfinished in their eagerness to test out Becky's theory in the field. Here, again, we see academic and amateur (and female and male) readings of landscape coming into dialogue—not for the first time, Lance and Andy are confronted with the fact that other ways of seeing and of knowing the landscape might matter just as much as their own—that deduction may, in fact, trump instinct.

Conclusion

The programme's first series ends with Lance, Andy, Becky, and Sophie sweeping the High Field and finding nothing (except a ring pull—"'86. Shandy Bass", Lance confirms).[44] What the viewer knows is that Becky has read the clues correctly—this is the right spot—but, for now, the landscape is holding onto its secrets. What the protagonists cannot see (that which lies beneath the surface of the landscape) we can; as the camera —what the shooting script calls "Treasurecam"—moves down below the surface of the soil, it reveals "the grave goods of a rich Saxon ship burial: gold and garnet sword pommels, buckles and clasps, intricately decorated shield bosses and a beautiful Saxon warrior's helmet".[45] This is truly Deep England. As the detectorists call it a day and head for the pub, a wide drone shot takes in the view from High Field to the church below and beyond to the sun setting on the horizon. As the camera moves up, we see, traced on the grass, the unmistakable outline of a large ship—its prow facing west. Here, it is the viewer who becomes, momentarily at least, the reader of the landscape; its clues sufficiently obvious and unambiguous from this aerial perspective so as to make us wish we could call Lance and Andy back, to let them see what we can see: their destiny, waiting silently in the landscape.

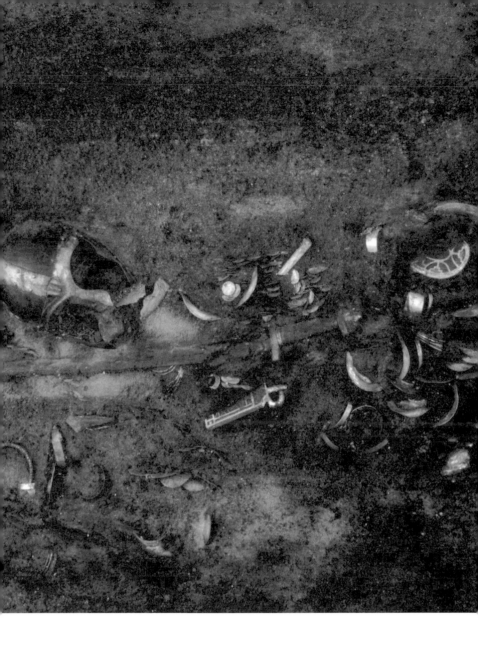

"The grave goods of a rich Saxon ship burial"

"That's a retaining plate from the back of a mid-twentieth-century socket mount"

Isla Forsyth

Hoarding the everyday— the disquieting geographies of the *Detectorists*

1. Mark Wallace, 'Being a Detectorist has its Moments to Treasure', *The Guardian*, 2 January 2015: theguardian.com/commentisfree/2015/jan/02/being-a-metal-detectorist-has-its-moments-to-treasure
2. Ibid.
3. S3, E1, 3:10. / 4. S3, E1, 3:21. / 5. S3, E1, 3:25.
6. Mary Shepperson, 'The Tense Truce Between *Detectorists* and Archaeologists', *The Guardian*, 18 December 2017: theguardian.com/science/2017/dec/18/the-tense-truce-between-detectorists-and-archaeologists
7. Shepperson, 'Tense Truce'.
8. David Harvey, 'Broad Down, Devon: Archaeological and Other Stories', *Journal of Material Culture* 15, no.3 (2010): p.348.
9. Ibid., p.357.
10. Ibid.
11. Wallace, 'Being a Detectorist'.
12. S3, E6, 26:35, 26:39.
13. John Harries, 'A Stone that Feels Right in the Hand: Tactile Memory, the Abduction of Agency and Presence of the Past', *Journal of Material Culture* 22, no.1 (2017).
14. S2, E1, 5:25.
15. Joe Moran, 'History, Memory and the Everyday', *Rethinking History* 8, no.1 (2004): p.62.
16. Tim Edensor, 'Mundane Hauntings: Commuting Through the Phantasmagoric Working-Class Spaces of Manchester, England', *cultural geographies* 15, no.3 (2008): p.313.
17. Moran, 'History, Memory and the Everyday': p.54.
18. Þóra Pétursdóttir, 'Concrete Matters: Ruins of Modernity and the Things Called Heritage', *Journal of Social Archaeology* 13, no.1 (2013).
19. Caitlin DeSilvey, 'Observed Decay: Telling Stories with Mutable Things', *Journal of Material Culture* 11, no.3 (2006): p.324.
20. Gísli Pálsson, 'Situating Nature: Ruins of Modernity as Náttúruperlur', *Tourist Studies* 13, no.2 (2013): p.175.
21. Moran, 'History, Memory and the Everyday': p.56.
22. Ibid. p.58.
23. Ibid. p.61.
24. Caitlin DeSilvey, 'Salvage Memory: Constellating Material Histories on a Hardscrabble Homestead', *cultural geographies* 14, no.3 (2007): p.422.
25. Gary Blackwell, '*Detectorists*—Reviewed by an Actual Metal Detectorist', *i*, 15 May 2017: inews.co.uk/culture/television/detectorists-reviewed-metal-detector/

Like all the best hobbies, detecting rests on a "central streak of futility"; the vast majority of the detector's beeps are merely digital traces of submerged modern litter or scrap metal corroded and decayed beyond identification.[1] For journalist and detectorist Mark Wallace, "you only find that [truth] out by digging a hole to reach your latest disappointment".[2] It is this aspect of detecting—the inevitable surfacing of modern, everyday litter—that this chapter takes as its focus, considering the materiality of the not-too-distant past or, perhaps more accurately, the not-so-distant present. Such ordinary remnants of contemporary life resurface regularly, dashing the detectorists' hopes that a piece of History will reveal itself; they chide us with the reminder that, in pursuit of the extraordinary, it is the everyday that we are most likely to encounter. Recovering the familiar, albeit dislocated, detritus of the everyday does, however, hold the potential to unsettle the ordinary, the seemingly unremarkable, by bringing attention to how little time is required for the remnants of lives to be scattered and dispersed without context or memory.

In the first episode of the third series of *Detectorists*, Andy hands Lance a piece of rusted metal he has just unearthed and asks what he thinks it could be. With confident certainty, Lance replies: "That's a retaining plate from the back of a mid-twentieth-century socket mount."[3] "Brilliant. I can cross that off my wish list", Andy mutters sardonically.[4] The mundane hoard of the metal detectorist is an uncanny collection of objects resurrected after their loss or disposal. It is the afterlife of such objects—and their persistence beyond the point of use or value—that leads the detectorists' hoard to be at once cathartic, in layering the present into time and place, and melancholic, in unearthing sites abandoned and pasts buried. Recovering such objects is also unsettling, as the present's seeming permanence is confronted with its inevitable transience. *Detectorists* offers a meditation on these disquieting geographies because it forces us to imagine landscapes through their forgotten everyday histories and we are reminded that the present, and our own lives, will inevitably disintegrate into shards of buried objects, echoes of a thousand ordinary moments, mundane activities, and unremarkable routines. A retaining plate may not be Roman gold but, as Lance reminds Andy, "Don't knock it, mate. That's a piece of history right there. Small scrap of a life long forgotten."[5]

Situating the everyday

Metal detecting emerged as a post-war hobby in Britain when relatively cheap portable detectors that had been developed for the army began to be made available to the public.[6] The number of hobbyist grew in the 1970s as detector technology became increasingly effective and affordable. Since then, detecting has—like so many British pastimes beyond the mainstream triumvirate of football, cricket, and drinking—remained a fringe hobby; a peculiarity spied from a car as it speeds past fields, or a curiosity encountered on a weekend country walk. Detectorists see themselves as amateur archaeologists, citizen-scientists democratising knowledge and enriching heritage. They are, however, often maligned by the professionals—archaeologists occasionally view the hobby as a nuisance or, worse still, an outright menace to the real work of history, as excavation sites are known to be tampered with, damaged, and looted by criminal metal seekers: the so-called nighthawks. For the archaeologist Mary Shepperson,

"The problem lies in fundamentally conflicting aims. Archaeologists primarily value *information* about the past. Objects are important, but only within their archaeological context—their relationship to structures, deposits and the full range of finds—contributing to the wider understanding of a site or landscape. For metal detectorists, the primary focus is the objects themselves, the collection of which by detectorists divorces an object from most of the information, which makes it valuable to an archaeologist."[7]

This division between archaeologist and detectorist—between located knowledge and divorced possession, between the processes of collating and classifying and merely collecting and amassing, between pursuing history and pursuing money—is perhaps unjust. It is certainly not the portrait of metal detecting

"Is that what I think it is?"

"Where are you going to put it all? Open a museum, eventually"

that we are shown in *Detectorists*. The programme presents the detectorist as a more rounded, more considered character: possessing a capacity for patience, a well of optimism, a wealth of detailed local knowledge, and a desire for a gentler pace of life.

The cultural geographer David Harvey has suggested that as archaeology has increased its range of theoretical and methodological positions and practices, it should also be "making space for some 'other stories'" and allowing for other storytellers.[8] In his study of the ritual landscape at Broad Down in Devon, Harvey demonstrates that the seemingly liminal figures and minor characters in the archaeological story of that site— including labourers and farmers—were essential to its history and its knowledge-construction process, yet have, in the main, been "airbrushed" from its past.[9] Harvey proposes that, by attending to the contributions of "these minor figures", we open ourselves to understanding landscape as a heterogeneous and relational set of practices and trajectories.[10] Such an approach sees value in the potential contribution of detectorists to narrating the history of landscape; a position than contrasts with Shepperson's somewhat unforgiving view of detectorists and their practices. That detectorists are not motivated solely by the potential material rewards of searching is made clear by the detectorist Mark Wallace:

> "For most of us, though, the true value of the things we find is human, not monetary. These are the relics not of famous kings and saints but of ordinary people. My finds tray… contains the belongings of individuals lost to history: the spur of a late medieval horseman, the small change of a Georgian farm labourer, the coin weights of a Stuart market trader. None of those original owners have a museum exhibition to their name, or even a name at all in the modern day."[11]

This sense of valuing that which might be overlooked in history's grand narrative—of caring for the small stories embedded in the landscape—is reflected in Lance's belief that the goal of the detectorist, in gathering up history's "scattered memories", is to "fill in the personality".[12]

The pleasure and excitement of metal detecting lies not in hunting for treasure *per se*, but in the prospect of uncovering a piece of the past—an object that instantaneously dissolves the distance between the centuries. The feeling of wonder in the moment of unearthing—when something which has long lain invisible resurfaces and, in that emergence, suggests the presence of another time and another life—and in doing so allows for an empathetic and intimate communion with the past.[13] Nevertheless, the bulk of what Andy, Lance, and the rest of the DMDC actually find, reinforces our sense that the majority of the detector's beeps and squeals do not facilitate a communion with the ancient past, but, rather, lead to the uncovering of everyday litter and a closer communication with the near present.

A hoard of everyday litter

Shot-gun caps;
Pennies;
Ring pulls—Tizer,
    Shandy Bass,
    Quatro (or was
    that Lilt?);
Buttons;
Buckles;
Badges;
Biscuit wrappers;
Drinks cans;
Nails;
Spoons;
Part of a trestle
    table;
Bit off a tractor
    (BOAT);

Part of a combine
    harvester
    (POACH);
Matchbox cars—
    Chevy Corvette,
    Pontiac Firebird,
    Ford Mustang;
Blankety Blank
    cheque book
    (sans pen);
Clay smoking pipes;
Barbed wire;
A *Jim'll Fix It* medal
    (quickly tossed
    and discarded);
Sweet wrappers;
A screwdriver;

Hot rocks and grots;
Tons of scrap metal;
The occasional
    piece of silver;
all turned over,
all resurfaced,
all in search for
the ultimate, and
illusive, treasure
—gold.

As this list of Lance and Andy's finds throughout the programme shows, much of their metal detecting is a process of unearthing and recovering everyday detritus. Most of what they find is that

"Ring Pulls Through the Ages"

"Pub? Go on then"

which makes up the material marginalia of ordinary lives: the boring stuff of doing, living, and disposing. Wading through the fragmentary, anonymous, generic, unowned, chucked, lost, taken-for-granted, and forgotten material remnants of the world can, however, occasionally prove dispiriting: "This isn't metal detecting", Andy complains in one episode, "This is scavenging on landfill".[14] That most of their finds are fragments of modern rubbish is not surprising—the temporality of their disposal means they lie much closer to the surface of the landscape than those more deeply buried ancient artefacts. Yet, their abundance is also indicative, as the scholar Joe Moran reminds us, of "a disposable culture in which the lifespan of technology and fashion is much shorter than the physical life of objects".[15]

In his work on industrial ruins, geographer Tim Edensor describes how the "speed of social and spatial change" means that "the contemporary era is a site of numerous hauntings".[16] These hauntings permeate sites and linger in the disposed objects of the everyday: drinks cans, loose change, scrap metal. Digging up these prosaic objects at the temporal distance of decades rather than centuries, confronts us with the realisation that the everyday is often void of historical significance because it is seen to be of the now—detritus of the endlessly repeating and routine task of maintaining and sustaining human life. These objects are, as Joe Moran explains, apparently "situated within dis-located, ahistorical time" and consequently "come to seem natural and inevitable, without origin or future direction".[17] A continual recovery of contemporary waste, the material remnants of a not-too-distant past, does not on first appearance seem to provide a moment to commune with the past. Yet, upturning a steady stream of the not-so-distant present indicates not only the volume of 'stuff' making up the banal mundanity of the everyday, but offers a moment to encounter our recognisable and tangible present passing into history.

Everyday litter reveals that our daily routines and rhythms are deeply embedded in assemblages that are not only spatially and temporally contingent but are also driven by (and inextricably entangled in) capital and political and cultural processes. Thus, if the everyday is continuously drained of historical meaning, *Detectorists* interjects and resists this ahistoricity by compelling us to reckon with the uncanniness of the not-so-distant present—a feeling not dissimilar to being confronted with an old photograph of yourself wearing, say, a 1980s shell suit, evoking a visceral memory of the feeling you had wearing it whilst simultaneously compelling a dispassionate review of an era now so unrelatable in its attitudes towards fashion, taste, and fire safety. We are, at once, both connected and detached from the image and the object. The detectorists' hoard of every-day litter offers an unsettling memory of a lived present revealed as a dated past or piece of unremarkable history.

Uncanny everyday artefacts

We can think of the detectorists' hoard of the everyday as uncanny, since the prosaic objects they uncover are altered and changed by a process of dislocation. Resurfacing without the context of use and belonging, the objects have the potential to disrupt the everyday. Without context these objects denaturalise their own once inevitable qualities, rendering visible and unsettling the illusion that our mundane everyday routines are somehow timeless. Dug up and laid bare, our ordinary activities are situated and located within historical processes. Like the modern ruin (which has captured much academic attention), the material remnants of the everyday come to occupy an unsettling space somewhere between disposal and history, or, in the case of the detectorist, between bin and finds table.[18] Scraps, remnants, and fragments when dug up and cleaned off become artefacts. *Detectorists* presents us with a procession of mundane artefacts, each a small testimony to overlooked routine practices, activities, and habits; unearthed objects reveal lives lived, lives forgotten, lives never acknowledged. The hoard of the everyday is uncanny, too, as the prosaic objects are altered and changed during their period of abandoned interment—variously mottled, clarty, dulled, rotted, and corroded. Cultural matter, in this sense, takes on an ecological form. Indeed, as cultural geographer Caitlin DeSilvey has noted, objects "have social lives, but they have biological and chemical lives as well, which may

"Scraps, remnants, and fragments when dug up and cleaned off become artefacts"

53

only become perceptible when the things begin to drop out of social circulation".[19]

Out of context and beyond utility, not only does the materiality of the everyday become visible, so too does its unstable nature, opening up possibilities for different histories and geographies to be traced and told. In describing the industrial ruins of a factory, for example, Gísli Pálsson captures the unsettling effect of the visible instability of objects from the not-so-distant present: "The creative participations between stone, moss, lichen, climate, stellar bodies, and so on led to growths and decay both biological and cultural… both aesthetically pleasing and viscerally disturbing."[20] Altered by earth and weathering, the materiality of the object becomes recognisably biological as well as cultural, its decay and rot is both grotesque and alluring. Its presence out of context, out of place, and out of matter are surprising and unsettling. Here, the cultural has been intruded upon, or, rather, the illusion of a precise, bounded culture has been exposed as a soothing fiction protecting and distancing us from the inevitable rhythms of the biological. If, as Joe Moran states, "the everyday is… significant because it is a sphere in which the modern and the residual can coexist", the materiality of the everyday of the detectorists' find is significant precisely because it reveals how the cultural and biological co-exist and are continually shaping, transforming, and changing.[21] As an object resurfaces, altered and uncanny, it reveals its nature and situates us as merely fleeting and superficial in deeper, longer temporalities. The discarded toy or broken trestle table are material testimony of our collective ageing and decay even within the mundane, inconspicuous, and seemingly timeless experiences of the everyday.

Conclusion

The detectorists' landscape of everyday litter represents a continual and gentle confrontation with transience and impermanence. As they pick through and turn over patches of earth, they churn up absence after absence after absence— objects without owners. Temporalities and materialities eddy and jostle, with no neat linear progression of time, space, or narrative. Like mediums calling forth near-forgotten and living memories, theirs is a spectral landscape of banal hauntings, which "explains the peculiar, inarticulable feeling of pathos experienced... when the anonymously functional is exposed as a product of time and an object of memory".[22] For Joe Moran, there is a "specific kind of sadness which attaches to these memories of everyday experience, as they puncture the myth of the timeless routine, and force us to contemplate the transience of unacknowledged lives".[23] Metal detecting, and the pursuit of treasures hidden, is for the most part a meditation on the fleeting nature of the present—a present that so swiftly becomes unceremoniously interred as shards of the past's everyday mundanity. The detectorists' jumble of junk, their hoard of everyday litter, opens up the possibility "to craft stories about people and place that might otherwise go untold".[24]

For detectorist Gary Blackwell, "Talking rubbish and finding rubbish while enjoying the great outdoors is part of the detectorist's everyday life".[25] *Detectorists* captures this spirit. The programme is an elegiac portrait of the prosaic, drawing attention to the pathos of the everyday. Infused with sharp humour and gentle melancholy, *Detectorists* reveals that lives once lived are only lives long forgotten if we do not make space or time for unearthing, for piecing together the small scraps and crafting rich narratives from the not-too-distant past and the not-so-distant present.

"So, you're all sorted? Visas and stuff? Jabs? All done. Ready to go. I've done nothing.
Becky's done it all"

Andrew Harris

"*When I get up it just goes to shit*"—unearthing the everyday vertical landscapes of *Detectorists*

1. *Detectorists* shooting script, S1, E1, 22 May 2014: unpaginated.
2. S6, E6, 13:46.
3. Tim Lewis, 'Mackenzie Crook: "We Aspire to Be the Sitcom Hardy Would Have Written"', *The Guardian*, 25 October 2015: theguardian.com/tv-and-radio/2015/oct/25/mackenzie-crook-the-detectorists-new-series
4. In its rural, ordinary, and archaeological concerns, *Detectorists* offers important and distinctive vantage points against work in an emerging field of vertical geography that tends to focus on explicitly militarised and securitised territories or densely configured urbanism. See, in particular, Stuart Elden, 'Secure the Volume: Vertical Geopolitics and the Depth of Power', *Political Geography* 34 (2013); Andrew Harris, 'Vertical Urbanisms: Opening up Geographies of the Three-Dimensional City', *Progress in Human Geography* 39, no.5 (2015); Stephen Graham, *Vertical: The City from Satellites to Bunkers* (London: Verso, 2016).
5. See Felicity Winkley, 'More than Treasure Hunting: The Motivations and Practices of Metal Detectorists and Their Attitudes to Landscape' (PhD diss., UCL, 2016): p.161.
6. S1, E1, 16:10.
7. Parch marks are ghostly pale outlines of former settlements that materialise on land when it dries out and grass and crops die off, particularly after heat waves. Writer Robert Macfarlane describes them as "aridity as x-ray, a drone's-eye-view back in time" in 'What Lies Beneath: Robert Macfarlane Travels Underland', *The Guardian*, 20 April 2019: theguardian.com/books/2019/apr/20/what-lies-beneath-robert-macfarlane
8. S2, E1, 19:03. / 9. S2, E4, 28:07; 28:26.
10. Eyal Weizman, *Forensic Architecture: Violence at the Threshold of Detectability* (New York: Zone Books, 2017).
11. Michel de Certeau, *The Practice of Everyday Life* (Berkeley: University of California Press, 1984): p.92.
12. Although not a detectorist, Sheila does seem to have more aerial nous than others. Her head-in-the-clouds persona seems also to convey 'heavenly' if not mystical qualities—a fact hinted at explicitly in the shot from above looking down on to her dancing to strange electronic music on her home record player.
13. S3E4, 1:33. / 14. S1E6, 1:55. / 15. S3E4, 2:10. / 16. S3E4, 2:26. / 17. S3E4, 2:34.
18. Nadia Bartolini, 'Rome's Pasts and the Creation of New Urban Spaces: Brecciation, Matter, and the Play of Surfaces and Depths', *Environment and Planning D: Society and Space* 31, no.6 (2013).
19. S3, E1, 3:53.
20. Xan Brooks, 'Road to Nowhere: The New Crop of Writers Unearthing the Dark Side of Village Life', *The Guardian*, 3 March 2018: theguardian.com/books/2018/mar/03/rural-retreat-dark-side-village-life-detectorists-this-country-lie-land-reservoir-13
21. S3, E1, 12:10. / 22. S6, E1, 1:10. / 23. S1, E4, 11:27. / 24. S1, E2, 21:06. 25. S1, E2, 21:09. / 26. S2, E6, 1:47. / 27. S2, E6, 5:04.
28. Christmas Special, 20:12; 4:33.
29. Christmas Special, 9:14.
30. Hito Steyerl, 'In Free Fall: A Thought Experiment on Vertical Perspective', *e-flux journal* no.24 (April 2011).
31. Nigel Clark, 'Politics of Strata', *Theory, Culture & Society* 34, no.2–3 (2016).
32. BBC Writersroom, 'Mackenzie Crook on Writing, Performing and Creating BBC Four's *Detectorists*', 19 November 2014: bbc.co.uk/blogs/writersroom/entries/7ab3598a-8acb-30c9-a6e5-ec062dec4216

The first series of *Detectorists* opens with a static landscape shot of "two stooped figures... some distance apart" approaching each other slowly across a flat, ploughed field whilst sweeping the earth with metal detectors.[1] In this establishing shot, the programme sets out its core focus: two middle-aged men, Lance and Andy, and their search for archaeological, financial, and personal treasure in the English rural landscape. This is a world framed by the relationship between detectorists and the ground immediately beneath their feet. The third series, in contrast, begins not with fields, oak trees, and bucolic meadows buffeted gently in the breeze, but with an overhead tracking shot that moves across the gleaming skyscrapers and densely packed urban landscape of the City of London. This scene of iconic towers, viewed from above, is seemingly a world away from detectorists in the Essex countryside with their "coils to the soil".[2]

This chapter argues, however, that there is a close and restless relationship between these two contrasting perspectives in *Detectorists*. Although detecting for metal involves patiently scanning the Earth's surface, the programme and its protagonists demonstrate how these actions are bound up with—and in turn unsettle—relations and connections both above and below the ground; this is an activity that involves more than simply walking across fields in a horizontal direction. The opening sequence of the third series is, in fact, more earthbound and ordinary than perhaps first appears. Not only is the City of London a landscape richly layered with history stretching back to the Roman era, but the most prominent skyscrapers featured in the initial aerial shot—the Walkie-Talkie, Cheesegrater, and Gherkin—have names that would not be out of place in Lance and Andy's everyday life.

The entangling of different vertical perspectives in *Detectorists* was, in some senses, there from the programme's inception. Reflecting on its origins, Mackenzie Crook recalls that *Detectorists* "was born a long way from the stubbly, golden fields and ancient landmarks of Suffolk", finding its genesis during his time filming the sci-fi drama *Almost Human*:

"I'd been writing these snippets of conversation between these two characters, talking absolute rubbish, out in a field… It was odd to be writing those scenes living on the 25th floor of a glass skyscraper in downtown Vancouver. But it seemed to work—maybe because I was longing to get out of there."[3]

Detectorists can, in this way, be understood as a reaction to shiny, corporate, high-rise landscapes—albeit one framed from experiences of condos in the sky. The closest the programme gets to vertical stacking, beyond the opening shot of the third series, is the massed vegetable crates in the depot where Lance works as a forklift driver and the piled-up boxes of DMDC fleeces that Lance has delivered in his aborted bid to become club president.

This chapter investigates the intricate relationship in *Detectorists* between height and surface, and above and below—a relationship that offers a way of exploring three-dimensional imaginations and experiences of contemporary Britain.[4] The chapter begins by considering both the value of aerial perspectives in understanding the ground below and their capacity for misinterpretation. I then probe layered histories beneath the surface and assess difficulties faced by the programme's protagonists in evaluating an opaque and unreliable earth below. The final section of the chapter returns to the default, ground-level orientation that, like the opening to the first series, defines the detectorists' practice, investigating how at the emotional and physical heart of *Detectorists* is an inherent groundedness.

Grounding the aerial in *Detectorists*

Consulting maps and aerial photographs in order to second-guess where potential ancient hoards and other hidden nuggets might be found is common practice for detectorists.[5] The aerial approaches used by the DMDC include consulting historical photographs of bomb craters (this to help Peter, the apparent *ingénue* German tourist, locate his grandfather's aeroplane,

"The closest the programmes gets to vertical stacking is the massed vegetable crates in the depot where Lance works"

shot down during the Second World War), and interrogating the topographical detail provided by an Ordnance Survey map of the local area in Becky's explicitly geographical efforts at locating the possible site of a Saxon ship burial. More up-to-date digital techniques are also adopted. In episode one of the first series, while looking at Google Earth with Lance over a mid-week vegetable curry, Andy reports he has been doing some "recon"; he points out a straight road running up the side of a farm that he suggests could be indicative of Roman activity.[6] The shot that opens the next episode—sweeping down from a blue sky to Lance and Andy detecting on the ground below—hints at the logic these two detectorists have followed: moving from Google Earth's remote perspective to an actual engagement with the earth of this farm.

Detectorists shows, however, how a reliance on cartographic and digital views from above is inevitably accompanied by misinterpretations and disconnections. For instance, what sparks the detectorists' online recce is Lance's eagerness to show Andy a startling find on Google Earth of what appear to be parch marks with ring-shaped features that have become visible following what he describes as "the hot, dry summer we've had".[7] Andy is quick to spot a potential glitch in Lance's interpretation: he has mistaken the Google Earth watermark for an iron-age roundhouse. Whilst this elementary error of not distinguishing the proprietary digital watermark from the rest of the Google Earth map might seem inconsistent with Lance's extensive general (sometimes geeky) knowledge about political speeches, ring pulls, medieval history, tyre marks, and *Blankety Blank* episodes, amongst other topics, it is consistent with how new digital mapping technologies, despite their increasing accessibility, are not always straightforward to use effectively, especially for someone, such as Lance, who admits he is "not very good with the email".[8] Lance and Andy both also fail to realise that the Google Earth images would not necessarily show any parch marks from that summer anyway given they are likely to be several months, if not years, old.

There are other junctures in *Detectorists* where access to place-based digital knowledge also breaks down. In one of Lance and Andy's numerous TV-orientated conversations, the subject of *The Wombles* comes up—appropriately so, given that this is another British television programme centred around its protagonists navigating between the surface and sub-surface in search of that which has been lost or discarded. When Andy expresses doubt that the Wombles' home on Wimbledon Common is a real place—even when Lance carefully explains that the "fictitious Wombles lived fictitiously on the real-life Wimbledon Common"—he is encouraged by Lance to "Google it", but there is no signal out in the field, even with Andy holding his phone up to the sky.[9] This lack of reliable internet connection might seem incongruous given the importance of this part of East England for military operations, yet, beyond their camouflage fleeces and late-night stakeout efforts, the detectorists are not integrated into the wider war-machine, complete with its sophisticated aerial visions and surveying technologies. Indeed, in the second episode of the first series, two fighter jets roar rapidly overhead while Lance and Andy, heads down and headphones on, obliviously and unsuccessfully search the ground. In the third series, Paul and Phil (aka 'Simon and Garfunkel') attempt to use a drone to spy on their rivals, Lance and Andy, but fail to fly it properly and it shoots up out of view before crashing back down to earth.

Even aerial surveying undertaken with greater expertise is subject to inherent and perhaps convenient limits. At the start of the third series, a large colour aerial photograph of Church Farm is rolled out onto a desk in the City, as Photon Harvest present to financiers on their plans for a new solar farm outside Danebury. The camera starts spiralling down onto this image and it is transformed into a real-time overhead shot. As the camera zooms down further, it becomes clear that one small dot on the aerial photograph is actually the distinctive Aztec yellow of Lance's Triumph TR7 car. As the shot drops down further still, in the manner of a Google Earth zoom, we see two figures striding across the field. This whole sequence not only helps illustrate the top-down control Photon Harvest now have over this area of land, but also demonstrates how important everyday details can be lost through the inherent limits to the resolution of aerial imagery. As with architectural theorist Eyal Weizman's forensic analysis of the way military aerial imagery is often at

"The camera pans upwards to reveal the clear outline of a longboat on the grass, a parch mark only visible to us"

a resolution that fails to make visible collateral damage from pinpoint drone strikes, Lance and Andy—and indeed the wider detectorist community—can be understood to be beyond the "thresholds of detectability" in Photon Harvest's conception and presentation of their new site.[10]

A stark illustration of the overall difficulties in securing full and effective aerial views occurs in the final shot of the first series. As members of the DMDC leave a field, resigned after yet another fruitless search, the camera pans upwards to reveal the clear outline of a longboat on the grass, a parch mark only visible to us, the viewer. Despite their surface-level detecting efforts, and Becky's topographical analysis suggesting that this could be the potential burial site, the detectorists miss this extensive hoard right beneath their feet even if its potential presence is obvious from only metres above them. Ultimately they do not have sufficient access to this higher perspective—what cultural theorist Michel de Certeau refers to as the "solar Eye"—and the treasure below is over their heads.[11] Perhaps the closest to the all-seeing eye in Detectorists is that possessed by the magpies who haunt the programme's third series, having stealthily and patiently accumulated a vast collection of gold coins.[12] Indeed, after one magpie steals a coin Lance has just unearthed, he speculates about catching one and strapping a camera to it. Not only do magpies seemingly possess superior knowledge from the air about what is happening on the ground, they also seem better placed in terms of understanding the relationship between the ground below and the historical shifts to which it has been witness. As Lance conjectures, "the magpies have been watching this spot for centuries, successive generations of them. The magpies know there's more down there".[13]

Lifting the ground in Detectorists

The opening of the second series introduces a novel component to the programme's portrayal of rural Essex. There are initially no signs of detecting, no gathering of the DMDC, and no sunlit fields, insects, or hedgerows. Instead, four horsemen appear on a horizon with chainmail and shields, their horses braying as lightning strikes in the twilight. Next, a monk in some distress is seen scooping up precious objects, including an aestel (the handle of a manuscript pointer), from a church and burying them in a sack in the fields beyond. The camera then drops beneath the surface to show the buried sack and, through a time-lapse sequence, we see the sack and other items disintegrate to leave only the gold and jewelled aestel. The camera then travels back up through the soil, deeper now with the passage of centuries, to show Lance and Andy with their detectors above, struggling to find anything below. This opening salvo to the second series is the first time a sense of the landscape's *longue durée* is directly represented. This notion of layered history, hidden below is nevertheless an aspect with which detectorists are acutely familiar. As with their efforts at using aerial views to tease out potential clues as to what lies beneath, the skill of the detectorist also relies on being able to assess how history is folded, often in strange and unexpected ways, into the ground beneath—especially in a location such as Essex, with a rich history of conquest and settlement.

A particular complexity involved in probing layers of history below results from potential discontinuities between depth beneath the surface and linear time. A logical assumption would be that chronological superimposition occurs, creating a palimpsest whereby the oldest artefacts are found further down. Andy, for example, is excited at the end of the first series when, following a strong signal from his detector, he has to dig down further than usual: "Jeez, this is deep. Whatever this is, it's been in there a long time."[14] Excitement builds further when "a glint of gold" is spotted.[15] Yet the object that is eventually exhumed is nothing more than a "fucking pound coin"—and one from that very year.[16] An incredulous Lance exclaims, "What's that doing nearly two foot under the ground?"[17] This incongruity clearly disrupts the detectorists' sense that the past is located in sequential layers downwards. Yet, as cultural geographer Nadia Bartolini argues in her research on buried material remnants from Rome's past, this assumption can be rather simplistic: "digging deeper does not necessarily imply an 'older' material past... in some cases depth does not correspond to linear time".[18]

"What's that doing nearly two foot under the ground?"

Given difficulties in establishing an effective longitudinal lens linking the supra- and sub-surface (without the benefit of TV special effects), as well as the encountering of often unexpected forms of historic temporal accumulation below, it is perhaps not surprising that the programme's most momentous unearthing occurs following a stimulus that is non-visual and not point-specific. At the end of the second series, Andy and Sophie are already leaving the field on their way to the pub after another unnoteworthy stint detecting. Lance lingers and hears distant horses' hoofs echoing up through the ages. This strange moment encourages Lance to make one last sweep with his detector, finding the aestel we previously saw buried, and precipitating the gold dance that climaxes the series.

Although such a moment where the buried sounds of history seep out into the open seems rather fantastical, Lance's acoustic and historical sensitivities to the landscape around and below him are signalled repeatedly. He frequently displays a close awareness of the presence of spectral forebears, for example musing at the start of the third series, "there's nowhere we could tread that hasn't been trodden on a thousand times before by Celts, the Druids, the Romans".[19] Indeed, Xan Brooks, in a *Guardian* review essay, posits Lance and Andy as "kindly mediums, in conversation with ghosts".[20] Lance is often shown to demonstrate an ability to listen carefully to the landscape, assisted in this regard by a lack of competing sonic life in his corner of rural Essex; as his prodigal daughter Kate observes, "This place is so deathly quiet at night, the tiniest noise… echoes around the town".[21] On one occasion, Lance returns to his flat and seems to hear something in the air. There is a sequence of jump-cuts from this scene, taking in progressively wider shots of the town, as if following the ripples of the sound Lance has heard. It transpires he has, indeed, heard something as his beloved TR7 comes into shot at the edge of town, being driven back by Kate having being borrowed for the weekend.

Given the stubborn resistance of the subterranean in revealing its historical secrets and artefacts, apart from those who strike lucky or show the patience and intuition of Lance, it is perhaps not out of the blue that the search for treasure in the final series, knowingly or otherwise, veers upwards and to the present and future rather than the past. This is most readily apparent in how, unlike in the first two series, a golden cache remains just out of reach of the detectorists directly *above* the ground they are searching rather than buried beneath it. The accumulation by magpies of coins up in the branches of a large oak is, moreover, an example of ongoing and active treasure hoarding rather than the one-off hoards deposited in the past that feature in the first two series. The magpies' stash of gold coins in the tree is, however, not the only treasure trove immediately above the detectorists' heads. This is explicitly indicated at the very start of the series by Photon Harvest's boardroom presentation:

> "For centuries, man [*sic*] has looked for the earth's bounty below the ground, but now we are on the brink of a new age of clean, carbon-neutral energy production from the sun—and the treasure, ladies and gentlemen, is very much above our heads."[22]

In the context of *Detectorists*, Photon Harvest's promised 'new age', can be understood not only in terms of challenging energy production's reliance on hydrocarbons accumulated in sedimented strata over geological time, but in disrupting the possibilities for locating historic human metal artefacts deposited in the ground. Photon Harvest's plan to cover Church Farm with solar panels, including removing shadow-casting trees, will have major impacts on both the detectorists, who will no longer have access to this piece of land, and the magpies, who have also been dependent on its historical secretions for satisfying their gold lust.

The groundedness of *Detectorists*

Despite competition from rival groups, magpies, and, indeed, solar energy for golden bounty, as well as difficulties encountered in accessing reliable knowledge about the ground—whether from aerial views or histories below—the detectorists, albeit with occasional wobbles, remain steadfast in their

"When I get up it just goes to shit"

commitment to their hobby. A key reason for this devotion to hours spent unearthing ring pulls, buttons, and scrap metal is not only the camaraderie enjoyed with other detectorists, but the escape the hobby offers from emotional complications above and beyond, such as employment woes and relationship troubles. Detecting offers a natural habitat where, in their regular donning of camouflage outfits, detectorists can meld into the earth and, as Andy half jokes, "hide from predators".[23]

The use of detecting as a defence mechanism against the inevitable challenges of the world beyond, revealed in the rich character stratigraphy developed for the programme's protagonists, seeps into the detectorists' everyday actions away from the field. A central example is Lance and Andy adjusting their bodily positions downwards in order to perform Lance's melancholic, thinly veiled song about his ex-wife, *New Age Girl*. While practicing in his flat, Lance admits that he cannot play his mandolin standing up but has to sit cross-legged on the floor: "When I get up it just goes to shit." When Andy tells Becky about their plans to perform the song at an open-mic night, she predicts he will be playing his guitar "staring at the ground".[24] After Andy refutes this, Becky continues: "You are always staring at the ground... you are always scanning the ground for stuff."[25] Here, Becky identifies the default ground-level stance with which detectorists seem most comfortable. Her predictions prove correct: Andy does stare at the ground through most of the duration of the pub performance whilst Lance plays cross-legged on a stool. Moreover, Andy takes on a sequence of temp jobs—grass strimming, floor polishing, line marking, and weed killing—that all ape the downward-glancing, ground-sweeping actions of detecting.

The instinctual ground-orientated habits of detectorists are a central feature in establishing the inherent groundedness of *Detectorists*. This is a programme that is, at its heart, down-to-earth, both in terms of the lack of pretensions of its protagonists as well as the physical connections they continually seek to make with the ground. As Lance revealingly notes, "Ambition's overrated. On TV, and all these people reaching for the stars. Striving to be the best. Looks exhausting."[26] Here, Lance not only continues his musings on a favourite subject of television, but demonstrates the way that he, and others in Danebury, are level-headed about their place in the world, preferring to keep their feet on their ground rather than unrealistically aiming starward. Given this earthbound preference, it is perhaps surprising that Lance lives in a first-floor flat. Lance's home, as with any building, is, however, physically connected to the earth below; the issue of its height above the ground only really arises when Lance is asked to visualise sinking down into its carpeted floor during a session at a hypnotherapist and immediately recognises the gap below. Indeed, Lance's reason for attending this session—his phobia of barges—might be understood not as a fear of going out onto water and its choppiness, imagined or otherwise, but of the lack of solid ground below.

Another key example of the importance of keeping to the ground occurs in the very last episode of the programme, when Phil climbs a stepladder in a collective erecting of the DMDC's new gazebo. Parched by the effort, Phil accepts a glass of Sheila's notorious lemonade (which Lance has already wisely turned down) and, seconds later, we see him tottering down to earth presumably unable to cope with its infamously sharp qualities. Although this might appear a continuation of a long-running infantile feud between these two, in many respects this was a gesture of Lance recognising and asserting Phil's new, more grounded status. Through experiencing Sheila's lemonade, Phil was inducted into the DMDC gang, and through falling off this high perch he was implicitly rescinding his previous claim, back in the first series, that "these amateurs [Lance and Andy] are beneath us".[27]

As well as placing due diligence on *Detectorists'* grounded-ness, a premium is also placed on maintaining the consistency of the ground on which these characters rely. For example, there is an important (albeit informal) code of back-filling any holes dug up during the course of detecting. There is also a keen sense of how removing significant items from the ground can disrupt a natural balance of forces, experienced by Lance when various unexplained mishaps occur after unearthing the aestel. Lance feels uneasy about how his find, "Mother Earth's secret", has now been taken to a closed cabinet-case on the upper floor of the British Museum: "It looks like a wild animal that's been

"Phil accepts a glass of Sheila's notorious lemonade and, seconds later, we see him tottering down to earth"

"*Detecting offers a natural habitat where detectorists can meld into the earth*"

trapped in a cage", he observes.[28] He is advised by club members that he needs to "reconnect to the land", and, after buying gold coins from an antiquarian shop and placing them in the soil, the apparent curse seems to be lifted.[29] Similarly, *Detectorists* closes with a scene showing items returned to their resting place. Although this final shot of the magpies' nest spilling out its coins down to the earth below seems significant for Lance and Andy collectively locating treasure after many false dawns, this is also important by concluding *Detectorists* with a moment when the historical ground is, temporarily at least, restored.

Conclusion

In its carefully regulated, self-conscious, and unashamed groundedness, *Detectorists* can be understood to run counter to a dominant sense in contemporary philosophy and visual culture of the way the ground below has fallen free; as the artist and essayist Hito Steyerl argues, "we no longer know whether we are objects or subjects as we spiral down in an imperceptible free fall".[30] Through its slow and careful attention to the mundane but extraordinarily rich world of its community of detectorists, *Detectorists* is seemingly able to arrest a sense of the conceptual and social ground being increasingly taken away from beneath us. This is not only in terms of being a programme that, against recent trends in British TV comedy, deliberately does not seek to undermine or mock its core characters, but in mining what many social scientists and geo-historians have recently argued is the potency of the geology below us in "looking 'upward' to the usual stomping grounds of human experience and agency".[31] This is all the more impressive given that, as Mackenzie Crook has revealed, "most of *Detectorists* was written standing up".[32]

"Becky is wholly present in Andy's hobby by dint of facilitating his capacity to undertake it"

Joanne Norcup

"That's got to be a first: woman reads map"[1]—gender, hobbies, & knowledge in *Detectorists*

1. S1, E6, 18:23.
2. Fiona Sturges, '*Detectorists*: A Rich Portrait of Unremarkable Lives Gone Slightly Awry', *The Guardian*, 9 December 2017: theguardian.com/tv-and-radio/2017/dec/09/detectorists-rich-portrait-unremarkable-lives-gone-slightly-awry-mackenzie-crook
3. Jim Reid speaking in *A Day Out With Detectorists* (2015): 5:51.
4. Alice Jones, 'Toby Jones and Mackenzie Crook on *Detectorists*: "When People Find it and Realise What it is, They Hold it Close to Them"', *i*, 7 November 2017: inews.co.uk/culture/detectorists-people-find-realise-hold-close/
5. See, for example, Lawrence D. Berg and Robyn Longhurst, 'Placing Masculinities and Geography', *Gender, Place and Culture* 10, no.4 (2003).
6. The phrase "man up" is used by various male and female characters throughout the series (for example, S2, E3, 11:15).
7. Teddy Jamieson, 'Face to Face: Mackenzie Crook on *Detectorists*, His Man Cave and Alternatives to Toxic Masculinity', *The Herald*, 9 November 2017: heraldscotland.com/arts_ents/15639339.face-to-face-mackenzie-crook-on-detectorists-his-man-cave-and-alternatives-to-toxic-masculinity/
8. Jamieson, 'Face to Face'.
9. S2, E3, 11:15; S2, E5, 22:11. / 10. S2, E3, 13:11. / 11. S1, E6, 13:53.
12. Such idealised visions of the male physique stem from historical examples of morally acceptable male bodies—the kind discussed in the lyrics of George Formby's (1937) *Biceps, Muscle and Brawn*.
13. S2, E2, 8:29. / 14. S1, E5, 13:57. / 15. S2, E4, 3:30. / 16. S2, E4, 3:33. / 17. S2, E6, 24:14. / 18. S2, E6, 24:18. / 19. S2, E1, 17:21. / 20. S2, E2, 2:07. / 21. S2, E2, 1:44. / 22. S1, E2, 10:42. / 23. S1, E2, 10:37. / 24. S1, E2, 10:45. / 25. S2, E1, 21:19. / 26. S2, E6, 20:26. / 27. S2, E1, 20:04. / 28. S2, E1, 22:33. / 29. S2, E1, 24:02. / 30. S1, E3, 23:55. / 31. S3, E1, 23:18. / 32. S1, E6, 24:40.
33. Rachael Dixey, 'The Geography of Leisure: A Gender Perspective', *Contemporary Issues in Geography and Education* 3, no.1 (1988). For commentary on women's art and the relegation of craft, see Rozsika Parker, *The Subversive Stitch: Embroidery and the Making of the Feminine* (London: Women's Press, 1984) and Rozsika Parker and Griselda Pollock, *Old Mistresses: Women, Art, and Ideology* (New York: Pantheon Books, 1981).
34. See, for example, Cheryl McEwan, 'Gender, Science and Physical Geography in Nineteenth-Century Britain', *Area* 30, no.3 (1998) and Avril Maddrell, *Complex Locations: Women's Geographical Work in the UK 1850–1970* (Chichester: Wiley-Blackwell, 2009).
35. David Matless and Laura Cameron, 'Experiment in Landscape: The Norfolk Excavations of Marietta Pallis', *Journal of Historical Geography* 32, no.1 (2006). See, also, Briony McDonagh, *Elite Women and the Agricultural Landscape, 1700–1830*, (London: Routledge, 2018).
36. S2, E3, 12:53.

"*Detectorists* is about nothing and everything. Made with palpable love, it's about people and their passions; camaraderie and community. As a portrait of male friendship, it is closer to documentary than drama, delving beneath the topsoil of mid-life ennui via the sparsest of exchanges."[2]

For Fiona Sturges, there is much to celebrate about *Detectorists*—a sitcom that conveys humanity, humility, and humour in its examination of the small yet significant moments in the lives of a community of hobbyists. For Jim Reid, executive producer of *Detectorists*, the programme "represents a slice of... British life—the sort of middle ground. You know, the people in it, they're not yobs, they're not aristocrats, they're not careerists, they're not geniuses, but they're not stupid and they're decent people... And a lot of British people who perhaps aren't so good at expressing themselves emotionally, like going out in a field on their own, or in their garden shed, and getting on with their hobby—they're not harming anyone."[3] In framing a programme around the marginal hobby of metal detecting, Mackenzie Crook and his collaborators have crafted a comedy-drama that enables viewers to understand intimately the worlds of two middle-aged men: how their passions and dreams, ideas and ideals inform the practise of their hobby, shape their reasons for being, and colour the landscapes and lives they inhabit.

Viewers and reviewers have praised *Detectorists* for its attention to detail and for holding at its heart a depiction of "male friendship, and what it means to be a man".[4] This chapter extends that appreciation by foregrounding the programme's quotidian geographies of gender. By attending to the way male and female lives are performed and portrayed in *Detectorists*, I reveal other gendered geographies—in particular, the way gender informs how hobbies, knowledge, and landscapes are made and understood. Examining the diverse renderings of the programme's supporting characters—both male and female—reveals the contextually contingent, complex, and changeable ways gender norms are navigated spatially in a convincingly realised English rural landscape.[5] The depiction of gender roles in *Detectorists* serves, through gentle satire, to subvert toxic portrayals of what it means to be a 'man' or a 'woman', and to challenge the reductive knowledges that attempt to perpetuate and emplace those roles. This chapter considers, therefore, how characterisation, dialogue, and plotting in *Detectorists* together comment on gendered ideas of what it means to perform and make hobbyist knowledge.

"Man up"[6]—language and gender norms in *Detectorists*

> "*Detectorists* is a timely reminder that not all men are guilty of toxic masculinity. Yes, they might be rubbish at emotional articulacy at times, yes, they might be obsessed with things that don't actually matter in the long run (stamps, football, Roman coins). But they can also be caring, loving, committed. That's a workable masculinity, isn't it?"[7]

Discussions of—and tensions around—ideas of masculinities are a central theme in *Detectorists*, particularly for its male protagonists, Lance and Andy. For Mackenzie Crook, the nature of masculinity and male friendship was, in many respects, the programme's germ:

> "Early on, when I first started writing it [*Detectorists*], it was just these little snippets of bullshit conversation out in a field between Lance and Andy, exploring the way blokes talk to each other when their partners aren't around and not inhibited by having to be macho or masculine in the traditional sense… And you know what? I know I'm not masculine in the traditional sense. But I'm a good dad and a husband so surely that makes me a good enough man?"[8]

What it means to be a 'good enough' man—and husband and father—is a question explored both in the dialogue and interactions of the programme's characters and in the plotting of the meta narratives that run across the entire series. In what follows, I draw on examples from all three series of the programme to illustrate how the protagonists' ideas of gender shift as their lives and priorities change, and serve to alter the way they approach their hobby as a result.

Reflecting the prevalence of gendered language in everyday life, characters in *Detectorists* occasionally use pejorative gendered put-downs, articulating the ubiquitous way gendered language permeates even the smallest of interactions as an assertion of power. We see this, for example, when 'butch' lesbian DMDC member Louise insists that Russell "man up" when searching for the Mayor's chain of office (which has been 'misplaced' in a renowned dogging area), or when she is chastising Paul Lee—aka 'Simon'—after apprehending him during a stakeout of the crash site of a World War Two bomber ("Stop resisting and calm down, you big girl").[9] A similar, and repeated, putdown is used by Lance towards Simon and Garfunkel, whose arrival in the pub is greeted with the phrase "Evening ladies", to which Phil (aka 'Garfunkel') scornfully responds "yes, your catchphrase. It's really good, it's very amusing."[10] Efforts to undermine male characters in this way utilise the false idea that heteronormative femininity equates to incapability and that the female sex is innately weak or lacking. In the first series, when farmer Larry Bishop tells Lance and Sophie about the official activities taking place on his land, the gendered language he uses describes professional knowledge as a male domain: "They've all cleared off... The CID left when they realised there wasn't a murder, forensic boys went with them, and then the history chaps, the archaeologists, followed soon after."[11] The terms 'forensic boys' and 'history chaps' serve not only to position Bishop in a particular class and age context, but also compounds the casual, everyday patriarchal sexisms that omit the presence of professionally trained women who work in these fields and more generally the gendered bodies in which knowledge is perceived to be held.

Other assertions of essentialist heteronormative masculinity are present throughout the series, particularly with respect to the appearance and physicality of Lance and Andy and how they compare (or not) with an idealised 'rugged outdoor' trope.[12] Despite spending considerable time outdoors, both in his work and in his hobby, Lance is described by Peter—the assertive young German who features during the programme's second series—as being a "funny little guy".[13] Lance's belittled status is also illustrated in his awkward conversations with Tony, the local Pizza Hut manager and beau of ex-wife, Maggie. Tony is darker, broader, and taller than Lance, and is apparently unconcerned about verbally putting Lance down about his hobbies and his physical prowess. Tony is also possessed of socially acceptable masculine knowledge: in the pub quiz, which he attends with Lance and Maggie, he excels in questions about football and lads' mags. In Lance's candid summary, Tony—who does nothing to support Maggie financially, in the running of her shop, or helping to take her mum to the bingo—is "a cunt": self-interested and tolerating the presence of Lance only because Lance performs the elements of the relationship with Maggie that Tony does not want to do.[14] Once Lance realises Tony and Maggie are using him in order to access his National Lottery win, Lance sees them for the manipulative individuals they are.

Lance is not, however, an unmanly character; the assertion of his (albeit somewhat dated) maleness comes, most obviously, in the pride he shows for his Aztec-yellow Triumph TR7, his 'classic' Athena poster of a knickerless female tennis player scratching her bottom, his signed photo of 1980s page-three model and actress Linda Lusardi, and his wipe-clean cooking apron emblazoned with the body of a lithe young woman wearing a camouflage-patterned bikini (a nod both towards Lance's heterosexuality and his hobby). That Lance's flat is decorated with these items serves to position him as a man living alone and slightly out of his time—someone capable of maintaining the domestic sphere whilst also clinging to certain outdated markers of his gender.

Lance is seen to shift this position temporarily with the arrival, in the second series, of his adult daughter, Kate. When Lance says he wants to give a good impression, Andy offers up the advice to "hide the signed Linda Lusardi photo".[15] "It's already gone", Lance replies.[16] When Lance confides to Andy that he will no longer be listing "the life and career of Linda Lusardi" as a specialist subject on his *Mastermind* application, he is bemused that Andy would see it as creepy.[17] "Why would it be creepy?", he asks, "a bloke did Virginia Woolf last week".[18]

Nonetheless, Lusardi remains a constant ideal for Lance, eventually appearing in a dream sequence in the programme's third series in which she goes metal detecting with him, thus fulfilling a fantasy on two fronts. When Kate calls Lance out on his sexist and "degrading" Athena poster, Lance feigns ignorance, sidestepping the sexualised objectification—Lance is comfortable, more or less, with his own masculinity and sexuality. Whenever his own physical and sexual attractiveness is questioned, he is perplexed and defensive. This is exemplified in one scene where Russell mentions that internet dating caters for all tastes. Lance responds "are you insinuating I've strange tastes, Russell?", to which Russell replies, "not you, other people".[19] There is no suggestion that Lance feels sexually unattractive or inadequate, despite the putdowns he receives from Tony or Russell. Recalling the name of the old band he and Andy once had ('Fanny Magnet'), Lance is self-assured enough to believe his time— the moment of his peak attractiveness—is "right around the corner".[20]

Lance has a clear sense of male and female roles, and while not an overt chauvinist, nevertheless exhibits implicit awkwardness around women with academic qualifications or authority he himself does not possess. He uses the phrase "That's got to be a first" a few times in the first series; the 'joke' being deployed only after Becky or Sophie make statements that challenge Lance's own stereotyped understanding of the world: in Becky's case, her detailed and logically applied geographical knowledge in locating the likely site of Sexred's ship burial, and in Sophie's case, her status as a student and her close reading of Bede's *Historia Ecclesiastica*. In the programme's third series, when Lance's girlfriend, Toni, takes him to see a hypnotherapist. to help cure him of the seasickness he suffers on her barge, Lance double-takes when a young woman is introduced as Dr Hoffman. Lance proceeds to question Dr Hoffmann's methods throughout his session, revealing his distrust of her and her clinical practice, as much for her young age as her gender.

Andy, by contrast, is not as self-assured in his own masculine identity. Andy's 'less-than' stereotypical acceptable male physical appearance is alluded to and commented upon in passing by a number of the programme's characters, including Lance

"That's got to be a first: woman reads map"

who tells him that "back in the Tudor period, you might've been considered really attractive, you know, scrawny, the beard and the hair... stick a ruff around your neck, you could've been one of Lizzie the first's favourites".[21] On one occasion, Andy is questioned by a community police officer while waiting for Becky outside her school because he was "making mums nervous".[22] When Becky finally arrives, he asks her "do I look like a paedophile?"[23] Laughing, she offers the less-than-reassuring response, "well, you do have a bit of a look about you... I'd have said more drug dealer than paedophile".[24] Becky recognises this vulnerability and often teases Andy about it, like when she makes plans to go out after school with her colleague, 'Gay Martin', stifling laughter behind the fridge door when she tells Andy "oh he's not *gay*... it's an ironic nickname, because he's the least homosexual man you can possibly imagine. He's gorgeous, Spanish, all the women fancy him... I don't... But yeah, that's who I'm going out with."[25]

Becky's mum Veronica candidly tells Andy that she had always thought he was a "sad sack", but because Becky loves him, she values him.[26] In the second series, Andy is clearly a dedicated father to three-month-old Stanley; not only does he take Stanley metal detecting in a papoose, but he has also worked out a regime for him—"It's my own unique blend of teachings and I'm thinking of publishing it", he tells Becky.[27] When he attempts to give Veronica a rundown of Stan's routine, she is dismissive of his capabilities, kicking his timetable away from her doorstep while enquiring what he will be doing "whilst my daughter works and I look after Stanley?"[28] When Andy is later sat in the front of Lance's TR7, driving away from Veronica's house, he realises he still has 'Clothy'—the muslin Stan needs for his nap. Lance refuses to return, saying "He's three months old. Got to start toughening up."[29] Performing gender norms starts very young indeed and this joke is accentuated as Andy, holding Clothy, sucks his own thumb to comfort himself.

Despite her teasing, it is Becky's love of Andy that affirms his masculinity: she sees him as an idealist and dreamer with principles and ethics. Becky sees how they complement one another—he more wary and cautious, she more proactive and driving. As the main income earner of their household, it is

Becky who practically and materially makes their dreams a reality, working as a primary school teacher while Andy takes on temping jobs whilst studying part-time for his archaeology degree and pursing a hobby that complements his career goals. Despite having his head turned by the arrival of Sophie at the DMDC, and having a "pathetic, little midlife crisis", in the first series, Andy's most significant discovery across the programme's three series is that his real treasure is Becky.[30]

When Andy begins questioning his own masculinity in being able to protect his family if they go off to Africa in the second series, he is reminded by both Lance and Veronica that he *will* cope and find ways to achieve this by being himself. The final series sees Andy in his ideal job as an archaeologist, but the compromises made by the "dead behind the eyes" site manager, who is more concerned about delays to the scheduled office block construction than salvaging mosaic remains, leads Andy to quit on principle.[31] Andy tries to hide this fact from Becky, only to be spotted by Veronica (not) weed killing as an agency worker. When Andy comes clean to Veronica, she reminds him that Becky loves him because he has principles and ethics and that these are valuable traits. Both Becky and Veronica make Andy's dreams a reality when Becky bids at auction with money Veronica has loaned them for Andy's dream home, a tumble-down cottage with roses around the door. Andy's masculinity is thus validated. He is the stay-at-home dad; he is the home-maker (for hedgehogs, bats, and his own family), whose hobbyist tendencies enrich their lives. Andy embodies a way of being in the English countryside that lives close to and sustainably with the non-human lives that make the local ecology habitable for humans. That Andy is not ambitious by societal or corporate standards is attractive to Becky who, herself, wants a way to live an ethical and principled life.

By the end of the programme's final series, both Lance and Andy are valued for who they are, supported by the 'invisible' emotional and practical labours of the women in their lives: in Andy's case Becky and Veronica, and in Lance's by his daughter Kate (who majestically kicks Maggie out of Lance's life by quoting the film *Working Girl* at her), and by his mechanic-by-night, agricultural-college-student-by-day girlfriend, Toni.

"He is the stay-at-home dad; he is the home-maker (for hedgehogs, bats, and his own family)"

"Actually, Varde had an idea about that, didn't you?"

"You and your hobbies, I'll never understand men" —gender and hobbies in *Detectorists*

"She does understand that it's important to you. That's enough, isn't it? You don't need her to get into it. It's a hobby, that's all: men have hobbies and women don't understand them, that's the way it's always been. I mean, how many female trainspotters are there? How many women commit to an afternoon reorganising their vinyl in alphabetical order? You don't want to spend an evening with a beautiful woman just comparing comic book collections, do you? What you want is your partner to shake her head, roll her eyes and look at you and say 'You and your hobbies, I'll never understand men'."[32]

Lance's monologue on hobbies answers, in part, Andy's unease that Becky cannot comprehend his hobby of metal detecting. What Lance fails to acknowledge, however, is that far from not understanding them, hobbies—and the related idea of spare or leisure time—have too often been an exclusionary prospect for women, especially those from socio-economically deprived situations where lower pay and lack of time restrict opportunities to regularly commit to a hobby. Where pastimes were deemed permissible for women, often moral, social, and cultural codes spatially prescribed these activities within the domestic realm (reading, sewing, cookery, gardening) or else in public institutions undertaking charitable work that often emulated female caring roles (volunteering in schools, care homes, hospitals, or religious institutions).[33] Women who wished to involve themselves with intellectually or physically stimulating hobbies out of doors were often met with gender barriers: either barred from joining learned societies outright or being more subtly excluded from them by having their capabilities scrutinised and perpetually questioned.[34] Where women did partake in clubs, learned societies, and institutions, it was often only because their class position meant that they had the benefit of time, finances, and social connections.[35] Women's participation did not, necessarily, equate to an acknowledgement of their capabilities and expertise—as such, many women are marginalised or silenced in official historical accounts of clubs and other social institutions. Thus, the idea that hobbies are the sole pursuit of men in their sheds (or in the outdoors) has an important historical gendered geography to it. *Detectorists* reflects (and responds to) this traditional silencing of women's voices in the portrayal of Varde, one of the few female members of the DMDC. Varde is a visible presence throughout the programme, but is (almost) always silent on screen. Although it is regularly implied that she is highly vocal in sharing her views and knowledge with club members, we typically only hear her contributions through the voice of other characters.

Lance's vision of hobbies as being a solely male pursuit, and women not understanding them, echoes what was clearly a disinterest felt by Maggie towards Lance's metal detecting. Lance acknowledges that Becky does understand that it is a hobby important to Andy and she never asks him to give it up, despite Andy's repeated misunderstanding that this is what she wants. Becky cannot commit the time Andy does to the hobby because, as a primary school teacher, she is seen to be working (as numerous educators do) well into the evening, restricting her 'spare time' to the occasional pub quiz, but it is in her capacity as the main wage earner that she allows Andy the time to study and to metal detect. Without Becky providing that support—as well as doing much of the invisible relationship work (writing Andy's CV, researching an archaeological position in Botswana for him, accepting the post on his behalf, and then organising all the visas, jabs, and travel arrangements)—Andy's prospects by the end of the second series would have stalled. Becky is wholly present in Andy's hobby by dint of facilitating his capacity to undertake it. For Lance, meanwhile, his position regarding women and hobbies shifts between the end of the first and second series. The arrival of Kate at the DMDC rally at the end of the second series sees Lance gift her a metal detector so he can introduce her to his hobby. That Kate—and, in the third series, Toni—attend club rallies to see with whom and what they are sharing him, reflects their support and love of him and his hobby.

Conclusion

Detectorists subtly subverts and critiques myopic normative representations of what it means to be 'male' or 'female'. The quotidian dramas Andy and Lance navigate as their lives and circumstances change, serve to reveal shifts in the ideas they hold about their own gender identities and to show that the practice of their hobby depends on broader networks and social relations that transcend their personal, professional, and leisure time. The men and women of *Detectorists* each have multiple identities that shift and change depending on their activities, and through their dialogues and discussions reveal they all have richer, deeper lives than this chapter has space to discuss. In focusing on the central male relationships between Lance and Andy, I hope to have shown how contingent their masculinities are on the relationships they have with the people in their personal and hobby lives. Male and female characters are made real: their complexities and capabilities are revealed and hinted at through the dialogue and discussions had with or around Lance and Andy. Far from being 'warm props' (or, indeed, "a minority"), the women in *Detectorists*—Becky, Veronica, Maggie, Toni, Kate, Sheila, Sophie, Louise, and Varde—are very much present, informing and facilitating the detectorists of the DMDC through their embodied knowledges.[36] The drama and tensions in *Detectorists* not only makes visible their presence in facilitating the hobby, and in enriching the public and private landscapes through which Lance and Andy are able to find their self-identity via metal detecting, but enable a humanity and humility to be revealed, giving glimpses of the diversity of women's and men's lives in Danebury, and, by turn, serving to acknowledge and celebrate the diversity of lives in the English rural landscape.

"They would have sailed the ship up the river to this point here, taken it out of the water, and brought it up the valley to this point... here"

Afterword

1. The third series was produced by Gill Isles, with Andrew Ellard serving as the story producer.

2. J. B. Harley, *Ordnance Survey Maps: A Descriptive Manual* (Southampton: Ordnance Survey, 1975).

3. For the second series, we turned to the even older Six-Inch County Series map to depict the area around St Giles, Henburystone.

4. S1, E4, 12:02.

5. S2, E3, 9:59; S2, E6, 25:10; S2, E4, 8:22.

6. Email from Adam Tandy to Mackenzie Crook, 11 December 2013.

7. On the camera recce, there was also nearly An Incident with a herd of cows in the same field. We will draw a veil over that experience.

8. Mackenzie and I both realised that you can't play exactly the same trick on the audience, so at the end of the second series the landscape is made to surrender its secrets, and on this second occasion the final drone shot is sustained by the victorious Gold Dance; Lance's discovery still brings joyful tears to my eyes.

9. S2, E2, 2:37.

10. To such an extent that comedy commissioners worry all the time that female characters are only ever written as shrewish nags. I think *Detectorists* demonstrates that if you write well enough, the 'strong woman' trope can be full of nuance and depth.

11. Auditioning the role of Varde was one of the most challenging casting sessions I have ever done; we asked actresses to listen to the scene being acted out, and then to show some—but not too much—interest. More difficult than it sounds.

12. A 'runner' in comedy is a series of thematically linked jokes, usually with an identical structure. In *Detectorists*, the best example of this is Andy's agency jobs, which consist largely of him walking along holding a pole-mounted device not dissimilar to a metal detector.

13. Email from Adam Tandy to Mackenzie Crook, 11 December 2013.

As the producer of *Detectorists* for its first two series and subsequent Christmas special, my job was to shepherd Mackenzie Crook's initial ideas into a shooting script and ultimately to deliver the finished programme to the screen.[1] Many people outside the film and television industry (and, indeed, plenty within) are unsure what it is that a producer contributes to the creative process. There are terms like director, writer, and actor that are probably better understood by outside observers but, in fact, the job of producer is integral to the realisation of the project. Sometimes the job is confined purely to raising money or to managing business affairs, but in scripted television the job is often editorial, and in television comedy this is particularly true. Comedy producers task themselves with preserving the creative integrity and value of the stories they set out to realise, protecting and clarifying the writer's vision, finding the right cast and production team, deciding on the right production methods, and then cheerleading the entire enterprise of bringing an idea to the screen in the most perfect way possible. The reality often involves a struggle to ensure that every contribution towards the endeavour is there on the day and happily fulfilling its role in precisely the right manner.

Another (albeit less kind) analysis might contend that this role is really just a licence to meddle in everyone's business— from the first draft of the script (and the second, third, and fourth drafts as well) to the precise sound of the hinges on the door of the DMDC clubhouse. But I like to imagine a producer is there to support, guide, and provide the creative glue that sticks everything together, or to offer an extra finger on the knot of the fancy bow. Quintessentially, the producer has to be a storyteller. So my response to the preceding chapters— written by all the 'Geography Degrees'—is purely from the perspective of a mere storyteller, and I am suitably grateful to all of them for the chance to comment on their contributions.

Romancing the landscape

Innes M. Keighren distinguishes two methods of picking out a story from a landscape: the application of technology and logic from the expert, and the passionate instinct of the pleb. We are often told these days that people in Britain have had enough of experts; that their gut tells them something different (and perhaps more palatable). So our detectorists rely not only on knowledge and expert guidance to read their landscapes, they will also act on hunches, rumour, and hearsay, which can be an incredibly useful tool for the storyteller. Note how often our amateurs abandon a piece of structured methodological research in favour of a wild hunch based on something they once heard in a pub, or "worked out" from reading *Historia Ecclesiastica*. Lance and Andy are certainly not picky about their sources: Charlie off of *Casualty* (despite, or perhaps because of, being the BBC's highest paid actor at the time) is as good as Bede when it comes to A-grade intel. But when those wild hunches turn up nothing more than a few Tupperware boxes of canine remains, our heroes are left with no recourse but to turn to the experts, in the form of Becky.

Faced with something that looks like a well-structured argument, full of informed interpretation, Lance and Andy reluctantly bow to the inevitable. In an earlier draft, the speech was given by Sophie, but I thought it was important for the analytical *coup de grâce* to come from Becky, both to ensure that she was properly invested in the final search for Sexred and because I think we had already decided that Becky's degree subject was geography, so it made more sense. However, given the amount of authoritative finger-pointing that Rachael Stirling wanted to do in performance, we were then tasked with the job of trying to place the landscape of our fictional burial story into the topology and topography of real Essex. This is why our 'Danebury' ended up being superimposed over the real landscape of Maldon, with a few judicious alterations by guerrilla cartographer Barry Sexton.

The obsession with maps in *Detectorists* is partly a product of my own delight in the printed representation of landscape, and I will cheerfully admit that it has been an interest of mine from a very early age (I'm pretty sure I was the only thirteen year old who begged to be given a copy of J. B. Harley's *Ordnance Survey Maps* for their birthday).[2] For the scene involving Becky's geographical reading of the Essex countryside, I selected from the Ordnance Survey's 1:25,000 First Series (Provisional Edition) in order to map our fictional Danebury. The small sheet size alone is enough to recommend it to an actor, as most folded maps are much larger and therefore much harder to work with as props. Moreover, the 1:25,000 First Series maps still have a hand-engraved look to them, unlike the majority of contemporary maps that are digitally squeezed out of a computer.[3] With our new prop map—'Danebury TL91'—spread out in the bar of our unit hotel, Rachael Stirling and I pored over the fictional countryside, working out how to fit the dialogue and landscape analysis to the map, in a bizarre inverse of the scene we were to film the following day, as a geographer, an historian, an archaeologist, and a fork-lift driver all walk into a pub...

The storyteller also has a third—and totally unscientific—method of divining story from a landscape: to draw on the forces of pure luck and blind fate. *Detectorists* more than occasionally enlists the forces of magical realism, where the sound of galloping horses or the song of a blackbird is used to represent the ancient spirits that have left their story and their treasure behind them. And in the third series, the ghosts are even more apparent. Magical forces can be more subtle and pervasive in the narrative than other plot mechanics.

Despite Sophie's apparent avarice—"Bollocks! Set it to 'treasure' and let's go get rich", she instructs Andy in the first series—and notwithstanding her conflicted motivations from the outset, she nevertheless brings good luck to Lance and Andy whenever she is present.[4] Andy has never found gold until he goes detecting with Sophie; she photographs him digging at the bottom of a rainbow, and within seconds he has unearthed his first gold coin. In the second series this theme is developed even further: Sophie points directly or indirectly to the location of the gold aestel on a number of occasions, whether indicating a location on a map, scratching a cross on the ground, or pouring away her tea.[5] Even the position of the rainbow design on the side of Peter's camper van arcs downwards, pointing to the treasure beneath Sophie's feet. I'm rather sorry that the character left town after her unhappy love affair with Peter; her powers of divination always came in very handy, even if the rest of the DMDC hardly ever noticed.

As storytellers, we get to decide what gets found and what doesn't, who uncovers the treasure and what and how they learn from it. After reading Mackenzie's first draft of the beginning of the first series, my initial reaction was that "if this was Hollywood Andy would get the girl and get the gold, but my hunch is that the right thing would be for Andy to get the girl and not mind that he's missed out on the gold".[6] My suspicion was that if we left the gold in the ground, BBC Four would come back for another series. And so we ended the first series with that God's-Eye perspective on the final search site, revealing the ploughed-away remains of the ship burial on the hill. This was the kind of shot that was rarely attempted in television comedy in 2014—requiring, as it did, the use of a drone and additional visual effects work—but it seemed to me an entirely necessary extravagance.[7] Ultimately, the landscape has pulled a fast one on our heroes, and yet they are still content to walk off into the sunset and happier futures.[8]

After the success of the first series of *Detectorists*, I pointed out to Cassian Harrison, BBC Four's channel editor, that BBC Four was basically invented to allow comedies to reference the Venerable Bede, so I was always very keen to keep the level of our factual background as geeky as possible. There was never room for everything to be included, however. Only Mackenzie and I ever knew the precise variant of the Junkers Ju 88 that crashed in the field, for example. It was a Ju 88 A-4, and so now you know too.

"If it hasn't been forgotten, I'm not interested"[9] —rich pickings in rubbish

Context is identified by Isla Forsyth as an essential difference between archaeologists and detectorists; between context and recovery. However, there are many types of detectorists with many different motivations, and the same is true of archaeologists. I am reminded of the two—albeit fictional—archaeologists in the film *Raiders of the Lost Ark* (1981): René Belloq and Indiana Jones. Both archaeologists are obsessive recoverers of artefacts without much interest in their context, but very much obsessed with their historical and mystical significance. There is little to be gained from speculating what *Raiders of the Lost Ark* would have been like if Indiana Jones had used a CTX-3000 instead of a whip. In a very early draft of *Detectorists*, Mackenzie Crook had introduced a sinister member of the DMDC who represented the 'dark side' of the hobby, but I think we dropped him when we realised that Simon and Garfunkel were more interesting as clownish antagonists. They better fitted the tone of the show we wanted to make, and a fully competent antagonist would have required us to increase the narrative stakes to the exclusion of some of our other themes.

Generally, our detectorists are not interested in easy pickings. They scorn the chance to detect on an old Victorian rubbish dump in the second series—the detecting equivalent of shooting fish in a barrel, rather than joining the hunt for elusive deep-water pike. But the ephemera that they inevitably find is also comedy gold for writers. Each of these reminders of our collective past is the trigger for a laugh of recognition. No-one had given a second thought to the wrapper of a Burton's Mint Viscount biscuit until Mackenzie came along. Or the absurdity of digging up a *Blankety Blank* chequebook (without pen), or the tragic bathos of a *Jim'll Fix It* medal. But we limited these type of finds to one or two a programme, or we too would have been guilty of plundering an old rubbish dump ourselves. This kind of joke can wear out relatively quickly, although sometimes we tried to make the anti-climax of the reveal hit all the harder by promising something quite exciting, before snatching defeat from the jaws of victory, as we did with the Status Quo badge in the second series. In unearthing the everyday, wading through the detritus of commonplace objects, we are actually examining our own lives, our society, and a constant reminder that every-one else's future contains our collective past. In *Detectorists*, aside from Lance's obsession with ring pulls, we suggest that, by contrast, the very best finds are not reminders of one's past, and not simply the decayed rubbish of our own lives, but real reminders of someone else's loss of a treasured possession, and the emotional connection to that person.

The vertical and the horizontal

The best comedy comes from truth, and it is entirely true that Mackenzie mistook the Google Earth watermark for an Iron-Age enclosure, just as it also true that it takes three remote controls to turn on the television in his house, a feat which is entirely beyond him but not his wife and children. Andrew Harris provides an extremely enjoyable analysis of the vertical worlds of *Detectorists*. I am intrigued by the idea of different modes of verticality. I began my afterword by making a claim to be a storyteller, and creating a story definitely involves its own verticalities. Proper stories have a depth to them that crawl down through space and time just like the long 'treasure-cam' shots in *Detectorists*. Their end expression—either as jokes, or plot, or sentiment—are often rooted in a complex subsoil of thoughts and ideas, most of which will never be seen or heard by the audience. But some emerge to prominence in the course of writing.

When I first thought hard about the character of Sheila, she was doing a trippy dance to some weird jazz music in her living room, but up until then she had just been the ethereal creature, slightly detached from reality, who came up with pithy put-downs in the DMDC meetings. But I began to wonder what it was that had made Sheila the way she was, and why Terry was so devoted to her; I really needed to know what the story was. Niggling away at this problem with Mackenzie in our script conferences, we uncovered the tragedy of a lost child, a couple's private grief, and their coping mechanisms. This seemed, in some senses, entirely unimportant as we wrestled with early drafts of the first series, but laying down that character's stratigraphy paid rich dividends when we were looking for the right character for Lance to open up to about his daughter in the second series. The resulting scene with Sheila in the pub garden is one of the most moving in the series, and it comes from creating characters with deep truths buried beneath their surface.

Andrew has identified the deliberate incongruity of putting Lance, the acrophobic, in a flat. Our location manager discovered that there were no purpose-built flats in Framlingham, which stood in for the fictional Danebury—it's an entirely horizontal community. We looked for a flat because that's what Mackenzie had written, and we ended up at the only split-level HMO in town, as far as we could tell. Its quirkiness was something we embraced, with a change of tenant every time we tried to work there. It also came with its own rather splendid aquarium, which clinched the deal for us. Tropical fish husbandry was an important part of Lance's character, and fish are difficult creatures to move around at short notice.

As a species we are horizontal by inclination, and wrestling with the vertical has always been a particular challenge on *Detectorists*, with our fondness for looking down on the landscape and investigating what lies beneath. These views from above or below are definitely the hardest bits to shoot, whether it involves the logistics of a drone shot with actors or action vehicles, subject to the vagaries of wind speed and cloud cover, or a camera position that peeks up out of a hole. The physical landscape is really *hard*, and several weeks were spent preparing the ground for our crew. No one wants to relive the pain and labour it took our art department to bury our 'neolithic' sarsen stone in the flinty high ground above the church in the second series. Our "Treasurecam" shots are clearly more a voyage of the imagination, almost like a cartoon journey to the centre of the earth, and these involved huge hand-carved blocks of expanded polystyrene which were painted and dressed with peat, cork, gravel, bark, and finally 'treasure'. By tradition, the location for these endeavours was the dangerously named Bomb Workshop at RAF Bentwaters and, once completed, these subterranean sets were carefully photographed by a scratch model unit, seconded from our main unit somewhere else on the base.

I think by the second series we'd realised it was actually far easier to shoot these vertical journeys horizontally, using motion-control cameras mounted above a set which could then be firmly anchored thereby allowing us to create the decay of time around the golden aestel. Half a dozen passes were done in slow-motion with the buried bible in various states of decay, creating fake history in the middle of the very real Cold War landscape of an abandoned USAF airbase. Finally, all the footage was composited together by the VFX wizards at Double Negative, with additional 'time passing' effects.

Mackenzie had been delighted by the success of our very first 'treasure-cam' shot, and wanted to give the audience an early tease of what was to come, right at the very start of the second series. However, simply seeing the gold aestel in its physical context didn't convey its narrative context. Poor old Sexred's entrance had been pre-announced as early as the very first episode, but the treasure in the second series had no such build-up. I therefore suggested we opened with a flashback that showed how the object came to be buried in the ground, and what the object actually was. Having laid down those layers of history, we gave the audience enough to realise where the story might be heading, and gave them weekly nudges with our opening titles for the second series.

Men (and women) and their hobbies

The men in *Detectorists* are, almost by habit, almost by choice, emasculated by strong, no-nonsense women. In this, the show shares some DNA with Roy Clarke's *Last of the Summer Wine*: men talk rubbish to each other, and fear the women in their lives. It is a not uncommon trope of British comedy.[10] The exceptions are those femmes fatales who represent the true threat to the status quo, by dint of their seductive powers. It is Sophie who unwittingly gets to fill this role in the first series and then gets to be played for a fool by Peter and the Dirt Sharks in the second. This is very unfair on Sophie as her only crime is to want to be involved with the men of the DMDC and their hobby of metal detecting. Joanne Norcup argues that women (and specifically women from outside the societal elite) are largely excluded from participating in hobbies, by various social and economic interventions. Whilst this is certainly true, the archetype of the male hobbyist is often a fairly pathetic figure, obsessed with the triviality of life—not necessarily someone with high social or economic capital. Men also recognise this as a truth, so I do not believe this portrayal is just propaganda spread by a few disaffected, excluded women. What is it about men that makes them choose to follow a hobby, to the point where it becomes character defining? Why should some men choose to define themselves by what they do with their leisure time, rather than what they do at their work, or, indeed, with their family? Perhaps, in previous times, it facilitated some kind of small escape from a daily existence that otherwise offered little variety. Perhaps, in these post-industrial times, where work and often family are harder to come by, hobbies now offer an escape from the *lack* of other social structures, and offer a means of masculine self-definition. The association between hobbies and masculinity provides a central character joke for Louise, who takes the expression of her own sexuality to extremes: taking the hobby of metal detecting extremely seriously, with the conviction that she can appear to be more masculine than her peer group of oddball men.

Aside from Sophie and Louise, one rather suspects the other women of *Detectorists* may only be humouring their partners, and that any feigned interest they exhibit is actually part of the very complicated courtship rituals between the archetypal metal detectorists and their partners. Certainly, that's true of Becky, and Sheila only attends the clubhouse meetings out of loyalty to Terry. Even Varde is initially only at the DMDC meetings out of loyalty to Louise.[11] By return, the men are often dismissive of the women's contributions to their world, for fear their masculinity will be further eroded. Lance's chauvinist joke to Sophie in the first episode—"That's got to be a first…"—was something that Toby Jones thought we should make a runner.[12] We enjoyed the crass awkwardness of the joke's construction, but we found it very hard to come up with variations while we were filming. Toby and I would try out ideas on each other during the shoot, but most of them just made us sound like dicks and were entirely unfunny. "Woman reads map" was an ad lib on the day we shot the scene in the pub (the line isn't in the shooting script), but I can't recall which of us offered it up.

Ultimately, Lance only affects to be comfortable with his own masculinity, surrounding himself with the trappings of a tabloid stereotype of what it is to be a man: pin-up posters, page-three girls, and pints. He is out of his depth when it comes to more complex aspects of what it is to be a man: unable to articulate his feelings for his ex-wife (series 1) and daughter (series 2) and finally both of them together with his new girlfriend (series 3).

His compulsion to continue seeing his ex-wife is the same one that leads him to stalk a previous ex-girlfriend (and probably not the chainsaw-wielding bed-wrecking girlfriend, I imagine), or buy presents for his absent daughter. He persists, even when confronted with Maggie and Tony having sex in the back of her shop and dutifully turns round the shop sign on Maggie's request as he leaves, despite his disgust both at them and himself.

While *Detectorists* does not mine the well-established trope of men-as-boys/women-as-adults in a straight-forward way, it does admit to celebrating a hobby that is so explicitly gendered and that its protagonists (mostly men) depend upon the love, or at least the tolerance, of the women in their lives in order to pursue their pastime.

Conclusion

Detectorists is a huge celebration of men and their obsessions, but is a celebration of other things too. The central theme of the series was the subject upon which Mackenzie and I most differed. If you were to ask Mackenzie, I think he would say that the series was primarily about metal detecting, men's love of hobbies, and why they do them. He was always keen to get lots of metal detecting into the storylines. I remember Mackenzie telling me that the "Men have hobbies and women don't under-stand them" speech was one of the very first he wrote for the series. But right from the start I thought

"*Detectorists* is about two men searching for their hearts' desire. Literally, the golden treasure of a Saxon ship-burial by following their on-the-spectrum Shed Man hobby. But that's mainly a very entertaining metaphor for their real searches for emotional happiness. Whether that's closure for a past relationship or a long-lost [daughter], or Andy realising that he's in danger of losing his ideal soul-mate because he's got his head down all the time, and can't see the best thing that's ever likely to happen to him is slipping away."[13]

Detectorists therefore became a rom-com almost by accident, although those elements were always there to be dug up from just below the surface. The first series pursued the theme of love and relationships, the second series love and parenthood. When we talked about doing a third series, Mackenzie pitched this extraordinary story of a family of magpies living in a tree for centuries, gathering ploughed-up gold. We discussed this notion of the birds' home being a secure and constant feature of a changing landscape, and I suggested that this should be the central theme of the third series—what it meant to have a home where one could put down roots. All of these themes are truly universal in their appeal, and perhaps this explains why a series about two blokes digging holes in the English countryside has become so loved by its audience.

Contributors

Innes M. Keighren is Reader in Historical Geography at Royal Holloway, University of London. He has research interests in geography's disciplinary and discursive histories, in book history, and in the history of science. He is author of *Bringing Geography to Book: Ellen Semple and the Reception of Geographical Knowledge* (2010) and co-author of *Travels into Print: Exploration, Writing, and Publishing with John Murray, 1773–1859* (2015). He is currently working on a new book focusing on the transnational reception of the eighteenth-century Scottish travel writer William Macintosh.

Andrew Harris is Associate Professor in Geography and Urban Studies at University College London, where he is convenor of the interdisciplinary MSc Urban Studies programme and Co-Director of the UCL Urban Laboratory. His research develops critical perspectives on the creative city and examines questions of vertical urbanism, particularly in Mumbai and London.

Joanne Norcup is Honorary Assistant Professor in the School of Geography at the University of Nottingham and Honorary Research Fellow in the Yesu Persaud Centre for Caribbean Studies at the University of Warwick. Her interdisciplinary research interests span cultural and historical geographies of knowledge-making, archives, popular culture, and public libraries. She is founder of Geography Workshop, an independent production company that has developed programmes for the BBC and Resonance FM. She is also a regular columnist for *The Beestonian*, where she writes about trees and sustainable allotment gardening. Her current research

focuses on questions of decolonisation and knowledge production in relation to the 1998 Royal Geographical Society (with the Institute of British Geographers) and British Council exhibition *Photos and Phantasms: Harry Johnston's Photographs of the Caribbean (1908–1909)*.

Isla Forsyth is Associate Professor in Cultural and Historical Geography at the University of Nottingham. Her research interests focus on military technologies and landscapes, desert and covert warfare, and the militarisation of nature. She is the author of *Second World War British Military Camouflage: Designing Deception* (2017). She is currently working on the history of spying in the Second World War and on the ethics of using biography and storytelling in the military archive.

Adam Tandy is the BAFTA-winning producer of *Detectorists*. He has produced several of the most significant British television comedy series of the past quarter century, including *The Armando Iannucci Shows*, *The Thick of It*, *The League of Gentlemen*, and *Inside No. 9*.

...

Mackenzie Crook is the BAFTA-winning writer-director of *Detectorists*. He has appeared in a wide range of both comedic and dramatic roles on television, screen, and stage, including *The Office*, the *Pirates of the Caribbean* film franchise, and *Jerusalem*. He has published two books for children with Faber and Faber and, more recently, has written and directed *Worzel Gummidge*, a television miniseries based on the novels of Barbara Euphan Todd.

Acknowledgements

We would like to thank the Historical Geography Research Group and the Social and Cultural Geography Research Group of the Royal Geographical Society (with the Institute of British Geographers) for jointly sponsoring the paper session upon which this book is based. The book's cover photograph, and all screengrabs from *Detectorists*, are reproduced by permission of Channel X, Treasure Trove Productions, and the individual cast members who feature in them: Orion Ben, Laura Checkley, Mackenzie Crook, Aimee-Ffion Edwards, Toby Jones, Divian Ladwa, Pearce Quigley, Rachael Stirling, and Sophie Thompson. We are grateful to Patrick Palmer at NENT Studios UK for his kind assistance in clearing the copyright permissions. The map of Danebury that appears on page 3 is reproduced by permission of Adam Tandy and the photograph of the book's contributors, which appears on page 107, is reproduced by permission of Alasdair Pinkerton.